D1531445

BY
MURRAY SCHISGAL

JIMMY SHINE

FRAGMENTS, WINDOWS AND OTHER PLAYS

THE TYPIST AND THE TIGER

LUV

Jimmy Shine

JIMMY SHINE

A PLAY BY

Murray Schisgal

NEW YORK ATHENEUM 1969

This play is the sole property of the author and is fully
protected by copyright. It may not be acted by professionals
or by amateurs without written consent. Public readings
and radio or television broadcasts are likewise forbidden.
All inquiries concerning rights should be addressed to the
author's agent, Janet Roberts, Ashley Famous Agency, 1301
Avenue of the Americas, New York, N.Y. 10019 (Bridget
Aschenberg—foreign).

TO JANE AND ZACHARY

FIRST NEW YORK PERFORMANCE

Brooks Atkinson Theatre, December 5, 1968

Jimmy Shine	Dustin Hoffman
Rosie Pitkin	Rose Gregorio
Elizabeth Evans	Susan Sullivan
Constance Fry	Pamela Payton-Wright
Michael Leon	Charles Siebert
Miss Green	Barbara Cason
Sally Weber	Rue McClanahan
Man in Closet	David Sabin
Lee Haines	Cleavon Little
Negro	
Gentleman	Arnold Wilkerson
Boy	John Pleshette
2nd Boy	Joel Warfield
Millie	Gale Dixon
Rita	Dorothy Emmerson
Boy Dancer	Johnny Evans
Girl	Kim Lang
Girl Dancer	Susan Segal
Mr. Lepke	Eli Mintz
Musicians	David Nichtern,
	Kenneth Altman,
	Michael Sachs,
	Irving Joseph

DIRECTED BY DONALD DRIVER

ACT I

The set is on three levels: an upper roof, running along the rear, with chimneys, a doorway leading down to the interior of the building and on both sides stairways leading down to the lower roof; on the left the lower roof is a large empty area and on the right it is no more than a platform in the curve of the stairs.

On stage level is a loft in a factory building that has been converted into a rather improbable artist's studio. Three or four steps lead from this to the lower roof, left; on the right the upper roof forms a bridge over a roof area; three washtub sculptured chairs, the one in the middle about four-and-a-half feet high, are downstage right; a large trash can is behind the stairs on the right; in front of the studio is a strip of roofing covered with tin.

The loft is a small room, with the entrance door at an angle, rear left; the bathroom door is beside it, rear. Along the left wall, an old gas range with pots and dirty dishes on it; next to it, a deep sink with a large keg of ice in it, around which are a great many cans of beer. In the rear, a rack filled with canvases. A pianola opposite the entrance door; in front of it, a bed; a single old bentwood chair; a telephone on the floor near the bed; newspapers and beer cans about the room; also a tin wastepaper basket.

JIMMY SHINE is seated against the headboard in bed, a hairy piece stuck to his bare chest. He smokes a cigar, drinks from a can of beer, tosses it into the wastepaper basket, listlessly picks up a newspaper and tries to read it; gives up, calls to ROSIE, who is in the bathroom.

JIMMY
[*Throws newspaper to floor; shouts*]

Hey!

[*No answer*]

Hey!

ROSIE
[*Offstage: shouts*]

Wha'?

JIMMY

You still in there?

ROSIE

No!

JIMMY

Come on out, huh?

ROSIE

Hold your horses.

JIMMY

How long you gonna be in there?
[*He gets up, wraps a bedsheet around him and goes to the bathroom door*]

ROSIE

Will you leave me alone a minute?
[JIMMY *opens the door.* ROSIE *slams it shut, screaming,* "JIMMY!" *She locks the door*]

JIMMY
[*Sulking*]

You're mad at me, aren't you?

ROSIE

I'm not mad at you.

JIMMY

You're mad at me. I can tell by your voice.

ROSIE

I'm not mad at you.

JIMMY

I'm rarely wrong about such things. Sooner or later everybody gets mad at me. It's been that way all my life. Hey!

ROSIE
[Shouts back from bathroom]

Wha'?

JIMMY

You coming out?

ROSIE

I'll be out! I'll be out!

JIMMY

When? Next year? What am I supposed to do here, all by myself? That wasn't the deal, Rosie. The deal was that you were coming up here to stay with me, in bed, all morning, that was the deal. But you didn't keep the deal. You're like all the others. You're a non-deal keeper.
[Knocks on the bathroom door]

JIMMY

Rosie!

ROSIE

What?

JIMMY

Talk to me!

ROSIE

What's there to talk about?

JIMMY

Anything. About anything. I'm going out of my mind here. I've been locked up in this room for a week and I'm not painting, I'm not working . . .
[*Plays Beethoven Fifth theme on the piano*]
Hanging around here, I'm getting so sick and depressed . . . Rosie!

ROSIE

What?

JIMMY

Talk to me.

ROSIE

Shh! Don't bother me now.

JIMMY
[*Bends down and looks through the keyhole*]
You're mad at me, aren't you?

ROSIE

I'm not mad at you.

JIMMY

Why are you shaving the hair under your arm?

ROSIE
[*Shouts*]
Get away from that door, Jimmy!

JIMMY

That's the only blade I have, so you'd better put it back
where you . . .

[*He pulls away from the keyhole, his eye covered
with shaving cream which* ROSIE *has "shot" through
the keyhole from a pressurized can*]

That's not funny, Rosie. I don't see anything funny about it.

[*He scoops shaving cream off his eye and his chest
piece*]

Aw . . . you ruined my fur.

[*He takes the chest piece off and puts it under the
pillow on the bed*]

ROSIE

[*Entering from the bathroom*]

OK. Wha' d'you wanna talk about? Pull up the zipper.

JIMMY

[*Doing so*]

You didn't hear anything I said before, did you?

ROSIE

Wha'?

JIMMY

Forget it.

ROSIE

Wha' did you say?

JIMMY

Forget it, Rosie. Just forget it!

ROSIE

What's the matter? You've been picking on me all morning,
I swear.

JIMMY

Picking on you! I'm trying to get some consideration, some sympathy out of you! Is that too much of one human being to ask from another human being?

ROSIE

[*She takes a mirror from the wall, leans it against the ice in the sink, and puts on her jewelry*]
Look, Jimmy, what I came up here to give you I gave you already, so how about payin' me so I can get outta here.

JIMMY

You'd leave me alone, wouldn't you? In my present state of mind, you'd actually leave me alone.

ROSIE

You can go out, who's stoppin' you? You're thirty years old; you don't have to stay up here all by yourself.

JIMMY

That's easy for you to say. You have places to go, business to take care of.

ROSIE

So find another job. What's the big deal?

JIMMY

You really have a heart of gold, don't you? You like seeing me loading furniture, running errands, chopping off fish heads. That appeals to you, doesn't it?

ROSIE

Why don't you go back an' paint? You got all your stuff up here. Painters make good money . . .

JIMMY

Because I'm not painting any more. Because I haven't painted
for a whole year. Because I got sick and tired of painting
bones. Bones, bones, bones.

[*Sings*]

"Dem bones, dem bones, dem dry bones, dem bones, dem
bones, dem wet bones . . ."

ROSIE

[*Takes a blond wig out of her large carry-all bag*]
You could make somebody crazy, I swear. I'm goin'.

[*Puts on the wig in front of the mirror.* JIMMY *goes
into the bathroom*]

Jimmy . . .

[*He re-enters with the can of shaving cream, which
he "threatens"* ROSIE *with; she jumps onto the bed*]

Cut it out, Jimmy.

JIMMY

Aha! I finally have you where I want you, Rosie Pitkin.

ROSIE

Never mind you finally have me where you want me. There's
the matter of the ten bucks you owe me from last time and
the ten bucks you owe me from this time . . .

JIMMY

I owe you ten bucks from last time?

ROSIE

Yeah, you owe me ten bucks from last time!

JIMMY

For what?

ROSIE

For what? For whatta you think!

JIMMY

Oh.

ROSIE

That's right.

JIMMY

I thought it was on the house last time.

ROSIE
[*Starts to put on a shoe*]
On the house? I never did anything in my life on the house!

JIMMY
[*Pulling her toward the bed on one foot*]
You wanna try?

ROSIE

No fooling around now, Jimmy. I ain't got all day. I got another appointment. Now will you just give me the money?

JIMMY
[*Lying on the bed*]
All right, Rosie, you can take any painting you want.

ROSIE

What do I want with a painting? If you don't have the money, why don't you sell that piano thing there? You could get a couple of hundred for it.

JIMMY

You really want the money.

ROSIE

Yes.

JIMMY

You went to bed with me for the money, is that it?

ROSIE

That's it.

JIMMY

No other reason.

ROSIE

No other reason.
> [JIMMY *sticks his thumb into his mouth and turns away from* ROSIE, *snuggling into the sheets.* ROSIE *shakes his shoulder*]

Jimmy.

JIMMY

Leave me alone.

ROSIE

I want my money, Jimmy.

JIMMY
> [*Sits up in bed, shouts*]

What's wrong with you? I'm dying! How can you keep nagging me about monetary remuneration?

ROSIE

I'm warning you, Jimmy . . .

JIMMY

All right, Rosie. If that's what you came up for . . .
> [*Pointing to his pants on the floor near the bed*]

There. The money's in the left-hand pocket. Take it and please go.

[*Starts to read the newspaper*]

We have nothing further of any consequence to talk about.

ROSIE

[*Turning the pants pockets inside out, one after another, all empty*]

Why are you mad at me for? I'm the one who should be mad. I have to fight with you . . .

JIMMY

[*As she searches*]

Take whatever you find in there. I don't care. It's not even worth discussing.

[*The telephone rings.* JIMMY *picks up the receiver*]

When you hear the dial tone, you will be disconnected.

[*He hangs up*]

ROSIE

Jimmy, if you don't give me the money . . .

JIMMY

What are you talking about? I told you to take it from my pants pocket.

ROSIE

Your pants pocket? There's no money in your pants pocket! Look for yourself!

[*She throws the pants at him*]

JIMMY

[*Wagging his head with feigned fury*]

Don't you pull that gambit on me, Rosie Pitkin! I've been around too long to be taken in by that swindle!

[*The phone rings again.* JIMMY *picks up the re-ceiver*]

Forty-third Precinct, Pickpocket Division . . . Who? Elizabeth? No, no, everything's fine. It's . . .

[*He gets up and takes the phone across the room as he talks*]

It's just such a surprise hearing from you, Elizabeth . . . Sure, sure you can come up . . . As soon as you can . . .

[ROSIE *starts taking off her shoes*]

That's right, top floor . . . I'll be waiting . . . Right.

[*He hangs up. To* ROSIE]

It was Elizabeth.

ROSIE

[*Starting to undress*]

I'm delighted.

JIMMY

She's coming here!

ROSIE

Oh, that's nice.

JIMMY

Rosie, you have to go. She's coming up. She'll be here.

ROSIE

Let's make love, Jimmy. You've aroused my appetite.

JIMMY

Rosie, please. You can't stay. Not now!

ROSIE

First you give me my twenty bucks, Jimmy.

JIMMY
[*Takes money from a can on the sink*]
Look, here's ten dollars. Come back in a couple of hours and
I'll give you the rest, I promise.
[*He is putting her shoes in her handbag*]

ROSIE
[*Trying to get her clothes back on*]
You're lucky I have another appointment or else I'd stay here
all day!

JIMMY
[*Throwing her out the door, half undressed*]
Go! Go! Keep your appointment! Rosie, you can get dressed
in the street. Have a good time!
[*He slams the door shut*]
Elizabeth is coming . . . My Elizabeth is coming . . .
[*He puts on a shirt which he takes from the stove.
He goes to the piano, plays the first eight bars of
Handel's "Harmonious Blacksmith." Then he
switches on the pianola, which plays a variation on
the Handel. And then a brass band does another
variation, with* JIMMY *jumping onto the bed, con-
ducting. And now the classroom voices of* MICHAEL,
ELIZABETH, CONNIE *and* SCHOOLCHILDREN *are heard
as they cross the upper roof from right to left and
enter the schoolroom, lower roof, left, singing the
school song. The sound of the schoolbell is heard.*
MISS GREEN *enters from the door, rear, lower roof,
carrying an attaché case, and sings along with them.
The pupils sit on the floor in three rows, one behind
another. (The actors here play children about thir-
teen years of age.) As soon as the song ends,* MISS
GREEN *starts to read the roll-book*]

MISS GREEN

Elizabeth Evans.

ELIZABETH

Present, Miss Green.

MISS GREEN

Constance Fry.

CONNIE

Present, Miss Green.

MISS GREEN

Michael Leon.

MICHAEL

Present, Miss Green.

MISS GREEN

James Shine.

JIMMY
[*In the room*]

Where's my shoe?

MISS GREEN

James Shine?

JIMMY

What did I do with my shoe?

MISS GREEN

James . . .

JIMMY

[*Finds the shoe, puts it on. Shouting*]

Coming, Miss Green. I'll be right there, Miss Green.

[*Enters, breathlessly, tucking his shirt into his pants, and sits on the floor*]

I'm here, Miss Green. Right here, Miss Green.

[*Present light in the loft dims*]

MISS GREEN

You're late again, James. Sit up. Sit up straight in your seat. Don't slouch. Now, this is the sixth time this month that you're late and unless you have an excellent excuse I'm sending you down to the Dean of the Boys!

CONNIE

[*Whispers to* ELIZABETH]

She's sending him to Mr. Hammerman.

ELIZABETH

[*Whispers to* CONNIE *over her shoulder*]

He's in very hot water now.

MISS GREEN

[*Loudly, turning* ELIZABETH'*s head back*]

To Mr. Hammerman! And you're getting a pink demerit slip. That will be your third pink demerit slip this term, which means you'll be suspended for the rest of the year. Now. What is your excuse for being late, James?

JIMMY

The truth, Miss Green?

MISS GREEN

The truth, James.

JIMMY
[*Loudly, boldly*]
A man was killed on Hinsdale Street!
[*The pupils whisper to one another, excitedly*]
It was a terrible thing to see, Miss Green. A horse went crazy and ran over him. There was blood all over the gutter, and his face, you should see where the horse's feet stepped on his face.
[*To pupils*]
It was twisted and torn and it was all out of shape and his guts were coming out of his nose!
[*The pupils make sounds and faces of repulsion*]

MISS GREEN
Was there anyone to help him, James? Was there a policeman?

JIMMY
There was a policeman, all right, Miss Green. He was the one sitting on that crazy horse!

MISS GREEN
And the man who was . . . injured?

JIMMY
I couldn't get a good look at him, but from where I was standing it looked a lot like . . . a lot like the Dean of the Boys!

MISS GREEN
[*Shocked*]
Mr. Hammerman . . .

JIMMY
[*Nods solemnly*]
Mr. Hammerman. There were pink demerit slips all over the
gutter, that's why I think it was him.
[*To pupils*]
He was covered all over with pink demerit slips; it was a
fantastic sight. There were trillions of pink demerit slips
falling . . .

MISS GREEN
[*Flustered*]
Excuse me, class. I'll be back shortly. Michael, pass out the
current-events pamphlets, please.

MICHAEL
Yes, Miss Green.

[MISS GREEN *exits, rear*]

CONNIE
[*To* ELIZABETH]
She's in love with Mr. Hammerman.

ELIZABETH
I was the first to tell you. Did you see her face turn white?

MICHAEL
[*Looking after* MISS GREEN]
She's gone.
[*To* JIMMY, *cynically*]
So Mr. Hammerman was hit by a horse.

ELIZABETH
Was there an accident, Jim?

JIMMY
[*Unable to lie to her*]

I . . . I got up late.

CONNIE

You take such chances. If Miss Green finds out . . .

MICHAEL

Let her find out. Who's afraid? This is more fun than writing
compositions, isn't it?

CONNIE

Isn't Mr. Hammerman married?

ELIZABETH
[*Nods*]

They'll probably get a divorce now.

CONNIE

Poor Mrs. Hammerman.

ELIZABETH

Why poor Mrs. Hammerman? She's much better off. Who'd
want a husband who was running around with other women,
especially someone like Miss Green?

MICHAEL
[*Seated*]

You can say that again. Imagine what it would be like having
a girl-friend like Miss Green!
[*He slaps his thigh, laughs aloud*]

ELIZABETH

What are you talking about? You don't have any girl-friend.

MICHAEL

No? As a matter of fact, I was out on a date myself yesterday.

JIMMY

A date?

CONNIE

What did you do?

JIMMY
[*Feeling slighted*]

Why didn't you tell me, Mike?

MICHAEL

I have my personal secrets.
[*To* CONNIE]

We went bike-riding, all along Linden Boulevard. It was
wonderful, great. She was sitting on the handlebars and I
had my arms around her . . .

BOY
[*Putting his hands over* MICHAEL's *eyes*]

Oh, Michael!

MICHAEL

Then we stopped and we sat down on the grass, behind a big
old tree . . .

CONNIE
[*Gaping*]

And what? What did you do?

MICHAEL

We . . . kissed.

BOY

Ecch!

[*He heaves as if vomiting and turns away*]

CONNIE

You kissed her?

MICHAEL

I did. And you know where?

CONNIE

On her . . . mouth?

MICHAEL

Directly and accurately under her proboscis.

JIMMY
[*Loudly and incredulously*]
You kissed her directly and accurately under her proboscis?

MICHAEL

Under her nose.

JIMMY

Oh.

ELIZABETH
[*Disdainfully*]
So what's a kiss?

JIMMY
Yeah, what's a kiss? Big deal.

CONNIE

Yeah. It's nothing. It's like kissing your hand. It's the same thing. There.

[*Kisses her own hand*]

I got a kiss, too.

MICHAEL

That's what you think. You're a bunch of ignoramuses. It's . . . different. She was wearing lipstick and it tasted like a delicious Chinese orange. And it's not only the kiss, it's what you do with it that counts. First you hold one another tightly, very very tightly . . . like this!

[*He suddenly grabs* CONNIE *into his arms. She screams*]

And then slowly, very very slowly, you bring her head around and up with the palm of your hand, like this . . .

[CONNIE *is trying to get out of* MICHAEL'*s tight grasp, screaming, "No!"* JIMMY *pushes her head up toward* MICHAEL'*s, then peeks under her skirt*]

And then you bring her face closer and closer . . .

[JIMMY *shifts around and looks up* CONNIE'*s skirt from another angle.* ELIZABETH *tries to push him away. The other children are laughing and screaming, all trying to get a better look at what* MICHAEL *is doing*]

Until your lips are almost touching, almost . . .

ANOTHER BOY

Here she comes! Here she comes!

[*The children scatter to their places and sit on the floor*]

MISS GREEN
[*Enters*]

On your feet, children.

[*They rise*]

Pledge allegiance to the flag.

[*They salute the flag*]

ALL

I pledge allegiance to the flag of the United States of America. And to the Republic for which it stands, one nation, indivisible, with liberty and justice for all.

MISS GREEN

Don't forget your assignment, children. We're having a history test on Friday.

[*The schoolbell rings. The children start to go*]

James, I want to see you a moment.

[JIMMY *moves to* MISS GREEN. *The others exit, noisily, chatting, carrying books*]

I saw Mr. Hammerman, James . . .

[*She puts on a pair of high-heeled shoes*]

and . . . I don't know what you hope to gain by lying, but, whatever it is, it won't work.

[*She has been pulling her stockings up at the thighs.* JIMMY *fidgets and turns away from her*]

James, I'm talking to you. Look at a person when you're spoken to!

[JIMMY *turns to her, shyly. As she takes her hair down*]

Why do you have to be so difficult? Why can't you be like Michael? He's your friend. Why don't you learn from his example?

[*Putting on a wide leather belt, unzipping her dress so that the neckline becomes a low* V]

Not only is he an excellent student, but he is an excellent draftsman. And that comes from diligence and application.

[*She hikes up her dress so that it rests above her knees*]

Now, I've warned you before, and this will positively be the last time. You are not going to go on to the next class until your work and conduct improves.

[*She closes her attaché case and starts to exit*]

You may go now.

                    JIMMY

Miss Green?

                    MISS GREEN
                    [*Turns to him*]

What is it?

                    JIMMY

You're some tomato!

                    MISS GREEN

James!

                    JIMMY

I didn't mean to say that, Miss Green; honest. I wanted to ask you how did I do on my spelling test?

                    MISS GREEN
                    [*Flatly*]

You failed.

                    JIMMY

Oh.

        [MISS GREEN *walks up the stairway, swinging her hips*]

Ohhh! Ohhh!

[*Shouting after her*]

I'll do better next time, Miss Green, I promise. I'll work on it.
I'll . . .

[*Mumbling to himself,* JIMMY *moves out of the
Set, back to his room*]

Failed. How do you like that? I thought I knew every word
by heart. I thought I was getting a hundred. Failed. F-A-L-E-D.

[*Back in his room, lights change to present time*]

Failed. Failed. Failed.

[*Claps hands*]

Elizabeth is coming!

[*Sings*]

Elizabeth is coming! Elizabeth . . .

[*He starts to straighten the room, putting beer cans
and newspapers in the wastepaper basket. Picks up
the sheet from floor, puts it on the bed. While
smoothing out the blanket on the bed, he sings*]

"When you walk with your girl down Cherry Lane . . .
Everyone is your friend, razzamatazz, razzamatazz . . ."

[*He covers the end of the bed with a dirty towel. On
the floor under the sink is a tin can of paint brushes,
with a baseball glove wrapped around it. As he puts
the can on the stove,* JIMMY *notices he is holding
the glove. As he smashes his fist into the glove a
couple of times, the lights change.* JIMMY *catches
and throws an imaginary ball as students come rush-
ing through on their way home from school. They
are now about fifteen years of age*]

MICHAEL

[*Tossing a ball to* JIMMY]

Hey, Jimmy! How'd you do on the algebra test?

JIMMY

I got ninety percent.
> [*They toss the ball back and forth*]

MICHAEL

Did you see my paper?

JIMMY

Yeah. You failed.

MICHAEL

Failed. I can't fail. It's impossible for me to fail. Haven't you realized that yet, Jimmy-old-friend? I've a natural inclination for the acquisition of knowledge.

JIMMY

Doody-doo.

MICHAEL

Yet I have no real desire to matriculate in college.

JIMMY

Doody-doody-doo.

MICHAEL
[*Sings*]

I'VE A NATURAL INCLINATION
FOR THE ACQUISITION OF KNOWLEDGE,
YET I HAVE NO REAL DESIRE
TO MATRICULATE IN COLLEGE.

JIMMY
[*Singing*]

YES, DESPITE OUR SPARKLING BRILLIANCE,

WE DECLINE TO JOIN THE MOB
AS THEY PROCEED WITH THEIR EDUCATION
FROM BEAST TO MAN TO SNOB.

                    MICHAEL
SO WITHOUT—

                        JIMMY
                        [*Trumpet*]
DE-DAH—

                    MICHAEL
—A QUALM—

                        JIMMY
—DE-DAH—

                    MICHAEL
WE HEREBY DO DECLARE

                        TOGETHER
WE'VE A NATURAL INCLINATION
FOR THE ACQUISITION OF KNOWLEDGE

                    MICHAEL
YET WE HAVE NO REAL DESIRE
TO MATRICULATE . . .

                        JIMMY
TO MATRICULATE . . .

                    MICHAEL
TO MATRICULATE . . .

JIMMY

TO MATRICULATE . . .

TOGETHER

TO MATRICULATE IN COLLEGE.

JIMMY

You're not kidding, Mike? You're really not going to college?

MICHAEL

Not me, no, sir. I've made up my mind. I'm not going to college. My parents want me to, naturally, but not me. Nope. I'm finishing high school and then I'm going to become . . .
     [*Starts up the stairs to the upper roof*]

JIMMY
[*Eagerly*]

What? What did you decide?

MICHAEL
[*Teasing*]

Ha-ha!

JIMMY

What, Mike? What are you going to become?

MICHAEL

An artist! A painter! A razzle-dazzle creator of the quintessence of nature, of color, of movement, of . . . of everything! That's it, Jimmy-old-friend. As soon as I finish high school, I'm renting a studio in Greenwich Village and I'm going to live there and work there and it's going to be great! great! great!
     [*He jumps down from the upper roof*]

JIMMY

Yeah, but what will you live on? Where will you get the money?

MICHAEL

I'll sell my paintings, what else, you silly old boob. I'll make a fortune. Do you have the faintest foggiest notion of what they pay for first-class proficient works of art? Thousands of dollars; more, even.

JIMMY

Boy, it sounds great, Mike, really great, but . . .

MICHAEL

But what?

JIMMY

But you have to learn how to paint, don't you? You have to go to school . . .

MICHAEL

So what? That's not the main thing. The main thing is that you have innate ability, talent, genius, something that's born inside you; it has nothing to do with studying. Some people got it; some don't. That's how it is in this cruel world.

JIMMY

Mike, do you . . .
                         [Takes a breath]
Do you think I got it?

MICHAEL

I don't know, Jimmy-old-friend. Can you paint?

JIMMY

I don't know. But if I could, that would really give me a
chance to do something, Mike, something beautiful.

MICHAEL

Well, let's see.
                    [*Gets off the swing*]
Let's not waste any more time.
                    [*Looks about*]
That tree over there. Paint it.

JIMMY

The tree?

MICHAEL

Paint it. Go on.

JIMMY
                    [*Takes chalk from his pocket; on his knees, he
                    draws a tree on the ground*]
I never did this seriously before, Mike. It'll be rough.

MICHAEL
                    [*Stands over him, strokes his chin reflectively*]
Tell me, Jimmy-old-friend, what do you see when you look
at that tree?

JIMMY

What do I . . .

MICHAEL

See. Visualize. Conceptualize. Is it a little old man . . .
or shadows and splashes of lights or . . .

JIMMY
[Shakes his head]
No. None of those things, Mike.

MICHAEL
Then what do you see?

JIMMY
I see a rotten old tree, that's what I see!

MICHAEL
Is that all?

JIMMY
That's all. Am I a failure?

MICHAEL
I'm afraid it doesn't seem promising.

JIMMY
[On his feet, kneading his hands, brushing back his
    hair]
Boy, I don't know what I'm going to do. I don't expect to
get into college. I have no trade, no connections . . .

MICHAEL
I don't want to be dogmatic, Jimmy. Your drawing of the
tree isn't that bad.
    [Looks at the sketch of the tree from another angle]
On second thought, I think . . . There might . . .
            [Suddenly emphatic]
There might be a chance for you, Jimmy Shine!

JIMMY
Do you really think so, Mike? Do you really think there's a

chance? Oh boy, that would be great! The two of us could
start together in Greenwich Village. It'd be great! great! great!
[JIMMY *has jumped onto* MICHAEL'*s back, throwing
his legs around his waist, holding him about the
neck.* MICHAEL *laughs and turns about.* ELIZABETH
and CONNIE *enter, holding each other around the
waist, whispering. They are wearing teen-age clothes,
carry books.* JIMMY, *embarrassed, slides down from*
MICHAEL'*s waist*]

CONNIE
[*Softly*]
Hello, Jimmy. Michael.

JIMMY
Hi.
[*Straightens clothes*]
Hello, Elizabeth.

ELIZABETH
[*Coming over to look at* JIMMY'*s drawing of the
tree*]
What are you two doing?

MICHAEL
We have things to discuss.

JIMMY
That's right.
[*He tries to rub out the drawing with his shoes as
he walks over it*]

ELIZABETH
What things?

MICHAEL

Private things.

JIMMY

That's right.
                    [*Ready to tell all*]
Mike and me just deci—

MICHAEL
          [*Clamps his hand over* JIMMY's *mouth*]
Don't tell them!

JIMMY

Right!

ELIZABETH

Who wants to hear? We have private things to discuss ourselves, don't we, Connie?

CONNIE

That's right!
                    [*They exit, giggling*]

JIMMY
          [*His eyes following the girls*]
Isn't she something?

MICHAEL

Isn't who something?

JIMMY

You know.

MICHAEL

Connie?

JIMMY
[*Grimaces*]

No, not Connie. Elizabeth. Elizabeth Evans. She's the most magnificent woman I've ever seen in my life.

MICHAEL

Then you haven't seen much, buddy.

JIMMY

You don't think she's magnificent?

MICHAEL

Not in the least. Her mouth's too big, she has a peculiar walk, and she has no breasts to speak of.

JIMMY

Elizabeth Evans has no breasts to speak of?

MICHAEL

No breasts at all. Or at best two underdeveloped tangerines.

JIMMY

Boy, you are blind. Like a bat. She's got terrific tangerines! And she's got everything else besides: brains, looks, personality . . . I just wish I had the guts to speak to her. But every time we're alone I get a bad case of diarrhea.

MICHAEL

A bad case of what?

JIMMY

Diarrhea! Didn't you ever get diarrhea!

MICHAEL

Not from Elizabeth Evans I didn't.

JIMMY

I do. Every time. As soon as we're alone together I have to
go to the bathroom.

MICHAEL
[*Seated on the stairs, right*]
Obviously she has a bad effect on you.

JIMMY

I don't know what it is. Once I met her on Jamaica Avenue
and I had to run three miles before I found a gas station.

MICHAEL

You were lucky.

JIMMY

I was lucky. Boy, was I lucky. It was closed!

MICHAEL

What did you do?

JIMMY

I knocked on somebody's door and I fainted.

MICHAEL

I don't see that you have such a problem, Jimmy. Next time
you meet Elizabeth Evans ask her if she'd mind speaking to
you in the bathroom.

JIMMY

When she's around I'm like a piece of steel filing and she's
an electromagnet. I get tense and all tied up. But you know
what I'd say to her if I could?
    [ELIZABETH *and* CONNIE *return, holding hands. They
    sit on the lower roof, left*]

I'd say, "Elizabeth Evans, you are the most exciting mystifying feminine personality I have ever seen. When I look at your eyes, I feel . . . I feel . . ."

MICHAEL
[*Rises*]
You feel what?

JIMMY
I feel sick, that's what I feel.
[*He passes* MICHAEL, *who grabs him by his belt. He struggles to free himself*]

MICHAEL
[*Indirectly to the girls*]
Well, it looks as if some people are more interested in some other people than they pretend to be.

ELIZABETH
This is a public park, Mr. Leon, and if some people wish to be here they have as much right as some other people who think that just because their parents have money the whole world has to bow down to them.

CONNIE
And besides I'm tired.

MICHAEL
I don't have the time to waste explaining to some people that my father built his business without the help or assistance of anyone and if some people's parents didn't do as well, then they didn't work for it, period!
[*To* JIMMY]
You coming?

[JIMMY *stares dumbly at* ELIZABETH. MICHAEL *flaps his hand disparagingly*]

I'll see you tomorrow. And remember what I said about tangerines. On second thought, seedless grapes!

[*He exits*]

ELIZABETH

[*Shouting after him*]

Good riddance, Mr. Leon! . . . I can't stand him.

CONNIE

Do you want to study tonight, Jimmy?

[*He shakes his head*]

ELIZABETH

[*Looks through the books on her lap*]

Oh-oh . . . Connie, will you do me a favor? I dropped my eco book somewhere and . . .

[*Rubbing her legs*]

my legs are so stiff from that gym class . . .

CONNIE

I'll get it. Sit there. Be right back, Jimmy.

[*She runs off*]

ELIZABETH

That's all I have to do is lose it. My parents would holler blue murder. What were you and Michael talking about that was so secret?

[JIMMY *is walking around the stairway, right, crouched almost in two, hands in his pockets*]

Jim, is anything the matter?

JIMMY

No, no, I . . . I have to go.

ELIZABETH

Don't you feel well?

JIMMY

I feel fine.

ELIZABETH

You are the most nervous person I know, Jim. You never
stand still. You're always doing something.

JIMMY

If you were in the predicament I'm in, you'd be doing something, too!

ELIZABETH

What were you and Michael talking about?

JIMMY

[Not moving about, one leg crossed in front of the
other]
College. We're not going. We're becoming painters. As soon
as we finish high school, we're renting a studio in Greenwich
Village, the two of us.

ELIZABETH

Why do you want to be a painter?

JIMMY

I'm not sure. But I think it's a chance to do something.
Something beautiful. If I'm good enough. I'd like to do a
painting of you, Elizabeth.

ELIZABETH

You would?

JIMMY
[*Nods*]

I'd really like to.

ELIZABETH

What would I wear?

JIMMY

A coat. I'd like you to wear a fur coat and a hat with flowers.

ELIZABETH

That'd be great. As soon as I get a fur coat I'll let you know.
[*Rises*]
I'd better help Connie look for my book. See you, Jim.
[*She exits.* JIMMY, *alone, goes back into the room.
Lights change to present time. He picks up the base-
ball glove*]

JIMMY

A fur coat and a hat with flowers.
[*He puts the glove away between some pipes that
run across the ceiling. Also stored there is a battered
portfolio, which he takes down, and blows the dust
off of. He sits on the lower steps, left, with the
portfolio, and opens it; inside, on top of drawings,
are a beret and a scarf which he puts on. Lights
change to past.* CONNIE *enters on the lower roof,
rear. She is seventeen years of age*]

CONNIE

Jimmy? Jimmy? Oh. There you are. I thought . . . Are you
sick?
[JIMMY *rises, shakes his head*]
Why didn't you come to school today?

JIMMY

I was busy; extremely busy.

CONNIE

You missed a lot of work. We're having our English Regents on Wednesday. If you don't pass that, you're not even going to finish high school.

JIMMY

Who cares?

CONNIE

Michael cares.

JIMMY

Like fun he does.

CONNIE

Like fun he does is right. He put in his application for college already.

JIMMY

You're wrong.

CONNIE

I saw it myself.

JIMMY

You saw it?

CONNIE

I saw it.

JIMMY

Mike can do whatever he wants. I'm going to be a painter.

[*Showing her a drawing in the portfolio*]
Take a look at this, Connie.

CONNIE

Jimmy, it's . . .

JIMMY

What do you think?

CONNIE

It's . . .
                    [*Suddenly*]
What is it?

JIMMY

What is it? Don't you know?
                    [*She shakes her head*]
It's a sketch of Elizabeth. Holding a bowl of wax fruit.

CONNIE

Elizabeth! Of course!

JIMMY

I did it from memory.

CONNIE

And there's a bunch of black bananas.

JIMMY
                    [*Pulling drawing away from her*]
That's Elizabeth's hand!

CONNIE

Elizabeth's hand, of course!
    [JIMMY *closes the portfolio and puts it under the
    bed*]

I knew it, Jimmy. What else could it be? I was only teasing
you.

JIMMY

I'm going to be an artist. That's set. That's definite. I'm
going to make something . . . beautiful. That's right, Constance Fry. Beautiful.

CONNIE

It will be. I'm positive, Jimmy.

JIMMY

[Chipping at the ice with a wooden mallet and an
ice pick]
And I don't care what anybody says or thinks. I'm not interested. I'm going to do nothing else, whatever happens. That's
my career. That's my future. And if I can't make it, if I
don't have it inside me, if I wasn't born with it . . .
[Throwing the ice pick into the floor, consciously
melodramatic]
then I know what to do.

CONNIE

Do what . . .

JIMMY

[Acting the movie psychopath]
Knives are incredibly fascinating to me, Constance Fry. I
find them the most fascinating objects conceived by the
human mind. See how it shines? See how sharp and clean
it is? It can cut a piece of bread and it can cut someone's
heart out just as quickly and easily.

CONNIE

You're scaring me, Jimmy.

JIMMY
[*Plucks the ice pick out of the floor and stands on
top of the sink, holding the ice pick high above him*]
When you stare at it long enough, you can't move your eyes
away from it. You're like a piece of steel filing and it's an
electromagnet. It has power and it can speak. It says, "When
you want eternal rest, Jimmy Shine, when all the cellular
tissues and vascular veins of your body cry out for complete
and absolute oblivion . . ."

CONNIE
[*On the verge of tears*]
Please put it away. Please.

JIMMY
[*Working himself into a false frenzy*]
It says to you, "It's time, buddy. Time to say goodbye,
goodbye . . . Time to lift the sacred knife of Montezuma
de Coolomacheba and, without fear or regret, plunge it
deeply . . ."
[*He makes fake plunges of the ice pick toward
his chest, muttering impassioned pseudo-Japanese
phrases*]

CONNIE
Stop it, Jimmy. Please, stop it!
[*She covers her face and sobs. As she runs out,
JIMMY calls after her*]

JIMMY
[*With a Japanese accent*]
Oh, Connie, I only make a jokee! Connie, you carry on like
a baby. Let me explain . . .
[*The lights change. As MICHAEL enters from rear,*

right, JIMMY *takes the scarf from around his neck
and ties it around his waist. They meet on stage-
level roof, down stage, center*]

MICHAEL

Let me explain, Jimmy, let me explain.

JIMMY
[*Peevishly*]

You don't have to, I told you.

MICHAEL

For cryin-out-loud, I haven't changed my plans.

JIMMY

You're going to college, aren't you?

MICHAEL

That's not the point. I made a deal with my father. After
I get my degree I can study art and he'll give me fifty bucks
a week to help me along. Fifty bucks, which means for the
both of us, buddy. And if things start getting rough, you're
going to be damn glad I had the foresight to make this
arrangement.

JIMMY
[*Sits downstage*]

But . . . I want to get out of the house now, Mike. You
said we were going to get a studio in Greenwich Village.
I don't have the money to do it alone, even if I got myself
a part-time job.

MICHAEL

Then wait. Hold on. You can paint at home. What's your
rush? It'll only be for a short while and then . . . we're off!!

We make the move together! And to show you I'm not entirely ungrateful for your cooperation . . . *voilà!*
[*He pulls a pint bottle of whiskey from his pocket*]

JIMMY

You didn't have to do that . . .

MICHAEL

I know I didn't, Jimmy-old-friend. But my generosity knows no bounds. Drink up, go on.
[*He sits next to* JIMMY]

JIMMY

Okay, Mike. You go to college . . . Lots of luck to you . . . I'll paint at home.
[*He drinks*]

MICHAEL

Now you're using your dome, Jimmy Shine.
[*Offers* JIMMY *a cigar*]
And once we're settled in and working, you can figure another year or two, and then, buddy, it's straight up to the top! Fame! Fortune! Crowds of people hanging around you, applauding and begging you to say a few words.

JIMMY

What do I say, Mike?

MICHAEL

[*Using the whiskey bottle as a microphone*]
I want to thank you for the money.

JIMMY

Yeah, yeah, yeah!

MICHAEL
I want to thank you for the broads.

JIMMY
[*Imitating the sound of a drum*]
Brrrrrrrr-pow!

MICHAEL
I'm here to show you my appreciation
For the ribbons and the awards.

JIMMY
[*He is joined by a real drum roll*]
Brrrrrrrr-pow!
   [*Singing to the banjo vamp and pantomiming play-
   ing a banjo*]
Ba-roompa, oom-pa,
Oomp-a, oomp-a . . .

JIMMY AND MICHAEL
[MICHAEL *joins the pantomime*]
Oomp-a, oomp-a, oom . . .
   [*And* MICHAEL *and* JIMMY *alternate singing choruses
   of a song as they tie beer cans to their feet and then
   jog up and down the tin roof*]

MICHAEL
[*Falsetto, with his hands in his sweater, miming
breasts*]
Oh, Mr. Shine.

JIMMY
Yes, Countess Leon?

MICHAEL

My husband just died and left me eleven million dollars and I'd love to become your patroness.

JIMMY
[*Puffing a cigar, imitating Groucho Marx*]
Once around the park, driver.

MICHAEL
[*Falsetto*]

Oh, Mr. Shine.

JIMMY

Yes, Countess Leon?

MICHAEL

I'm just crazy about your oils.

JIMMY

Oils? Wait till you see my tubes!
                    [*They sing a chorus of the song*]

MICHAEL
[*Pompous, miming a mustache*]
Mr. Shine. Mr. Shine.

JIMMY

Yes, Mister Park-dash-Bernet?

MICHAEL

Our gallery has never seen such enormous crowds for a one-man show.

JIMMY

That's because they've never seen one man show so much!

[*And they sing another chorus of the song.* MICHAEL *moves to the upper roof and goes into an auction-eer's spiel, ending with "Sold! An original Jimmy Shine!" as a crowd enters from all sides of the stage*]

MICHAEL

Who will start the bidding at two hundred? I need a bid of two hundred!

WOMAN

Two hundred dollars.

MICHAEL

Two hundred *thousand,* Madam.

JIMMY

Throw that broad out!
[*He hits a pot with a wooden mallet*]

GENTLEMEN

Two hundred thousand.

MICHAEL

Thank you, Monsieur Duveen.

MAN

Five hundred thousand.

GIRL

One million.

WELL-DRESSED LADY

One million, five hundred.

MICHAEL

Thank you, Princess Radziwill.

GENTLEMAN

Two million.

NEGRO GENTLEMAN

Two million, five hundred.

MICHAEL

Two million five, from the Organization of African Unity.

CHINESE LADY

Two million, seven hundred thousand.

MICHAEL

Thank you, Madam Chiang-kai-Check.

JIMMY

Check, hell, get cash.
 [*He hits the pot with the mallet*]

DISTINGUISHED GENTLEMAN

Three million.

BOY

Three million, two hundred thousand.

MAN

Three million, five hundred thousand.

LADY

Three million, seven hundred thousand.

WOMAN

Oh, sir . . .

JIMMY

Throw that broad out!
[*He hits the pot with the mallet*]

DISTINGUISHED GENTLEMAN

Four million dollars.
[*All gasp. The music vamp stops*]

WOMAN

That's more than the Rembrandt!

JIMMY

You bet your ass.
[*Hits the pot with the mallet. The music vamp starts
again*]

MICHAEL

Four million dollars. Four million dollars going once . . .
going twice . . . Sold to the Metropolitan Museum of Art
for four million dollars!
[*He drops the bag of money the* DISTINGUISHED GEN-
TLEMAN *has given him into* JIMMY's *pot. The music
vamp stops*]

NEGRO GENTLEMAN

Always the white man.
[*They all look at him. The music starts.* JIMMY
*throws the bag of money up from the pot and
catches it again; he lets it fall to the ground and it
bounces*]

DISTINGUISHED GENTLEMAN
[To JIMMY]
Between you and me, young man, what does it mean?

JIMMY
It's Aristotle contemplating Elizabeth Evans' bust!
   [*Another chorus of music.* JIMMY *tosses and catches
   the bag of money and then jumps onto the bed and
   lies down as the song ends. Lights change.* JIMMY
   lies on the bed, listening to the next conversation.
   ELIZABETH *and* CONNIE *cross the upper roof from left
   to right*]

ELIZABETH
You're making it up.

CONNIE
No. I'm not.

ELIZABETH
Swear?

CONNIE
Cross my heart.

ELIZABETH
A man exposed himself?

CONNIE
A man exposed himself. Right in front of everybody.

ELIZABETH
When did it happen?

CONNIE

Yesterday. In the subway.

ELIZABETH

Didn't anybody do anything?

CONNIE

It happened so quickly, I don't think anybody knew what was going on. He just did it, in a minute, then he ran off the train as soon as it pulled into the station.

ELIZABETH

How? How did he do it?

CONNIE

He had a newspaper on his lap, covering his . . . you know.

ELIZABETH

A newspaper?

CONNIE

The Wall Street Journal.

ELIZABETH

And then what did he do?

CONNIE

He just picked it up and smiled at everybody.

ELIZABETH
[*Slight pause*]

What did it look like?

CONNIE

Elizabeth!

[*They both start giggling and move off*]

ELIZABETH

I'm just curious . . .

CONNIE

I tell you, I was so embarrassed I turned all colors.

ELIZABETH

Was he good-looking?

CONNIE

Handsome. He was a handsome middle-aged man. Probably married and everything. It was the last thing I expected. . . .

ELIZABETH

I wish I'd seen it!

[*They exit, voices fading*]

JIMMY
[*Sitting up in bed*]

Mike!

MICHAEL
[*Entering from rear, right*]

Hey, Jimmy.

JIMMY

Let's go get fixed up at Sally Weber's.

MICHAEL

Sally . . . ?

JIMMY

Weber's.

MICHAEL

When?

JIMMY

Now. Right now.

MICHAEL

What's your rush?

JIMMY
[*Putting on his jacket*]
I've been spending all my time thinking about girls and
imagining all kinds of crazy things. I'm getting into bad
habits. I don't like it. Are you interested?

MICHAEL

No, no . . . I'm not in the mood.

JIMMY
[*At the foot of the stairs, right*]
Well, this is it, buddy.

MICHAEL

You sure . . . ?

JIMMY

I'm sure. I have to do it for my own peace of mind.

MICHAEL

Good luck, friend. Here.
                    [*Hands* JIMMY *a small tin*]
See that you protect yourself.

JIMMY

What's this?

MICHAEL

You know.

JIMMY

Oh.

MICHAEL

Use two of them.

JIMMY

Two of them?

MICHAEL

In case one breaks.

JIMMY
[Nods]

Thanks, Mike.
    [JIMMY *ascends the stairs, talking to himself. Lights
    out on* MICHAEL]
I'll be protected. Don't worry. I'll take every precaution . . .
    [He *turns to stare up at* SALLY WEBER, *standing mid-
    way on the upper roof. She is a slovenly woman in
    her thirties, unpainted, in a kimono*]

JIMMY

Miss Weber?
                    [Softly]
Miss Sally Weber?
                    [She nods]

I understand from certain friends and from something written
in the telephone booth at Julie's candy store . . .

SALLY
[Jerking her head]

Inside, lover.

JIMMY

Thank you, Miss Weber.

SALLY

Sit down. Get a load off your feet.

JIMMY
[Seated on a box]

Thank you, Miss Weber.

SALLY

Your first time?

JIMMY

The truth, Miss Weber?

SALLY

The truth.

JIMMY

I believe it is, Miss Weber.

SALLY

Your friend waiting for you outside?

JIMMY

Yes, he is, Miss Weber.

SALLY

Okay. If you want, Johnny . . .

JIMMY

Jimmy. Jimmy Shine.

SALLY
[*Smiling falsely*]
Jimmy. If you want, we could talk a few minutes, let your friend think somethin's goin' on up here . . .

JIMMY

Talk?

SALLY

Talk. Yeah. Then you could tell him what a real hot time you had up here an' how we . . .

JIMMY
[*Rises; loudly*]
Ohhh, no, Miss Weber. Ohh, no. I'm not paying you to give my friend phony baloney stories. My parents worked very hard for this money!

SALLY

Okay! Okay!

JIMMY

I came up here for peace of mind and I'm not leaving until I get peace of mind, I'll tell you that right now, Miss Weber!

SALLY

Okay. Hold your horses. You don't have t'bust a blood vessel.

You kids think everybody's out to cheat you. Okay, Johnny, let's . . .

[*She starts taking off her stockings*]

JIMMY

My name's Jimmy. Jimmy Shine.

SALLY
[*Smiling falsely*]

Jimmy.

JIMMY

I'm a painter, Miss Weber; a serious painter.

SALLY

Glad to know it.

JIMMY

I don't intend to go to college.

SALLY

That makes the two of us.

JIMMY
[*With inappropriate sincerity*]

I guess I'm making a big mistake but I don't have any choice now. You see, Miss Weber, I did terribly in high school. I failed five subjects. I failed French, I failed auto mechanics, I failed simple geometry twice . . .

SALLY
[*Shouts*]

Hey, will you do me a favor and keep quiet for a minute? I don't have all night to spend here with you!

JIMMY
[*Intimidated*]

Yes, Miss Weber.

SALLY

What kind of character are you?

JIMMY

I'm sorry, Miss Weber. What do you want me to do?

SALLY

Take your clothes off an' be quick about it.

JIMMY

Yes, Miss Weber.
[*Looks about*]
Isn't there supposed to be some kind of bed in here?

SALLY

There's a mattress in the closet. Now, will you get those clothes off so I can get done today?

JIMMY

Yes, Miss Weber.
[*Slight pause*]
What clothes do you want me to take off?
[SALLY *slaps her forehead and wearily runs her hand down over her face*]
I could take off all my clothes or I could just take off my shoes and socks.

SALLY
[*Facetiously*]
Whatta you wanna take off your shoes and socks for?

JIMMY

So I wouldn't dirty the mattress.

SALLY

That's very thoughtful of you.

JIMMY

Unless we didn't lie on the whole mattress . . . Our feet
would be on the floor.

SALLY

Look, why don't you wear what you want or take off what
you want, but whatta you say we go t'hell with ourselves and
use up the whole damn mattress!

JIMMY

Yes, Miss Weber.
                    [He guffaws lasciviously]
Miss Weber?

SALLY

What?

JIMMY

I decided to take off my pants.

SALLY
                    [She turns to him]
Congratulations.

JIMMY

Will you please turn around?

SALLY

Maybe you want me to leave the room?

JIMMY

No, no, you can stay, but . . .

SALLY

I could wait downstairs in the street and when you're ready
you can stick your head out the window and call me.

JIMMY

It's nothing personal, Miss Weber.

SALLY

I don't mind. I could even carry an umbrella under my arm
so you wouldn't call up the wrong person by mistake!

JIMMY

It's not personal, Miss Weber. I don't like it when anybody
watches me undress. I never let my mother watch me undress
either.

SALLY

She's a very fortunate woman.

JIMMY

It's my legs. I have terrible legs. I'd appreciate it if you didn't
laugh when you see them. I'm very sensitive about them.

SALLY

That is the saddest story I ever heard.
        [JIMMY *gives her an imploring look. She turns away.*
        He takes off his shoes and pants, then decides to
        hold his pants over his arm]

JIMMY
        [*Trying to be self-assured*]
I'm ready for you now, Miss Weber.

[SALLY *slowly turns toward him, like a prizefighter.
She removes her kimono. There are two large tattoos
on her arms. She stands in black bra and pants. She
swaggers to him, eyes him up and down, profession-
ally, boldly, laying it on thick*]

SALLY
[*Mouth twisted*]
Sure you don't wanna take your jacket off, lover?

JIMMY
[*With difficulty*]
No, Miss Weber. I have a slight chill.
[*He takes a handkerchief out of his pocket and mops
his face with it*]

SALLY
Are you ready?

JIMMY
Is there a bathroom in here?

SALLY
You can go to the bathroom later.

JIMMY
I think it would be better if I could go to the bathroom now,
Miss Weber.

SALLY
Hey, are you gonna . . .

JIMMY
I'm ready, Miss Weber.
[*Handing her* MICHAEL'S *tin*]

Do you get these or do I keep them?

[SALLY *puts the tin back into* JIMMY'*s jacket pocket.
She takes his hand and places it on her bottom. She
gestures for his other hand which holds his pants. He
puts the pants between his legs, puts his hand on her
bottom. She puts her arms around his neck*]

SALLY

Do you like me?

JIMMY
[*Nods fiercely*]

Mmmm!

SALLY

Is that all?

JIMMY

I think I'm in love with you, Miss Weber.

SALLY

Okay.

[*She pulls his pants away from him*]

JIMMY

Whoa!

SALLY

Get the mattress out of the closet.

JIMMY

Yes, Miss Weber . . . Darling.

[*He stares at her, moves backward to the upper-roof
door. He opens the door blindly, turns and sees a*

hairy *broad-shouldered* MAN, *with tattooed arms,*
wearing a rubber horror-mask, standing in the closet,
in undershirt, pants, no shoes or socks. The MAN
growls. JIMMY *screams, jumps back to* SALLY, *hug-*
ging her for dear life]

SALLY
It's my husband!
                    [*She pushes* JIMMY *out*]
Get outta here, quick, before he kills you!
         [JIMMY *runs downstairs, right, to the stage-level*
         roof. The MAN *emerges from the closet, removes his*
         mask. He and SALLY *break out in laughter, as she*
         gives him JIMMY'S *pants and he counts the money*
         in the pocket. SALLY *takes her clothing and exits*
         through the upper-roof door. The MAN *is counting*
         the money as JIMMY *calls*]

JIMMY
Miss Weber, will you please throw down my pants and
shoes? Miss Weber, will you please throw down my pants
at least?

ELIZABETH
                    [*Off*]
Jim!

JIMMY
Miss Weber!
         [*The* MAN *laughs and throws down* JIMMY'S *pants*
         and shoes. JIMMY *jumps into the trash can.* ELIZA-
         BETH *enters, calling*]

ELIZABETH
Jim?

[*Enters*]

Jim?

[*She peers into the trash can*]

Is that you, Jim?

JIMMY

[*Head slowly rising out of trash can; only his head
is visible*]

Hello, Elizabeth Evans.

ELIZABETH

What are you doing in there?

JIMMY

Yogi. I'm studying yogi. This is exercise fifty-four. It's called
"Contemplating Garbage."

ELIZABETH

How long do you have to stay like that?

JIMMY

Until the garbage man comes.

ELIZABETH

[*Laughs*]

You are insane, Jim. Completely insane. You're always doing
the weirdest things.

JIMMY

How are you, Elizabeth Evans?

ELIZABETH

Wonderful. Do you know I moved into my own apartment?

JIMMY

I heard you were working.

ELIZABETH

For a public-relations firm. They pay me over ninety dollars a week after taxes, and you've got to see my apartment. Two and a half rooms facing the river and it only costs eighty-five fifty a month.

JIMMY

I wish I could get out of the house.

ELIZABETH

Why don't you?

JIMMY

Because I can't take a full-time job. If I did, I wouldn't have time to paint; but as soon as Mike finishes college, we're renting a studio and sharing all expenses.

ELIZABETH

I think you're insane for waiting. Especially for Michael.

JIMMY

It's only two more years and I'm not just waiting. I'm developing a good abstractionist style, and besides, I'm getting a real confidence in my brush strokes.

ELIZABETH

Well, there's nothing like being on your own; you can take my word for that, Jim. I have to go. I promised someone at the office I'd have dinner with him. Come on, walk me to the bus stop.

JIMMY

Sure.

[*He picks up the can to his waist—it has no bottom —and starts walking with her*]

ELIZABETH

You're insane, Jim. Never mind.

[JIMMY *sets the can down again*]

Give me a good-luck kiss?

JIMMY

[*Kisses her on the cheek*]

Good luck, Elizabeth Evans.

ELIZABETH

Will I see you soon, Jim?

JIMMY

As soon as the garbage man comes.

[*She exits*]

I'll see you. I'll see you soon, Elizabeth.

[JIMMY *jumps out of the trash can, goes into his room. Lights change*]

Elizabeth.

[*Footsteps sound outside his room in the hallway. He puts his pants on quickly, calling*]

Elizabeth? Is that you, Elizabeth?

[*He goes out of the room into the hallway. Pause. He re-enters, opens a can of beer*]

Where is she? She said she'd be here. Where is she?

[MICHAEL *and* CONNIE *enter from the upper roof, right, laughing. Carousel music and amusement park lights. They come down the steps, right. They are about twenty-two years of age*]

CONNIE

Where is he? Didn't Jimmy tell you he was coming?

MICHAEL

He'll be here. I told him we'd meet him in front of the
parachute jump.

CONNIE

Sometimes he locks himself in his room and starts painting
and he forgets what time it is.

MICHAEL

He doesn't know how lucky he is. But one more month,
Constance Fry, and I'll be done with college and then you're
really going to see some painting!

CONNIE

There's Elizabeth! We're over here, Elizabeth!

ELIZABETH

Hi. Am I late? I didn't realize I had to change at Canal
Street. Good evening, Mr. Leon.

MICHAEL

Good evening, Miss Evans.

ELIZABETH

Where's Jimmy?

MICHAEL

He's coming. What are we standing around for? Come on,
let's do something.
                    [To CONNIE]
How about the roller-coaster?

CONNIE

I'll wait for Jimmy.

MICHAEL

Can I interest you, Miss Evans?

ELIZABETH

No, thank you, I'd just as soon wait . . .

MICHAEL

You're not afraid, are you?

ELIZABETH

Afraid of what?

MICHAEL
[*Half-smiling*]

It could be a certain person.

ELIZABETH
[*Returning his smile*]

That would be the day.

MICHAEL

Come on, then. Be my guest.
[*He grabs her hand and they run off, right, on the upper roof*]

ELIZABETH
[*To* CONNIE]

We'll be right back.
[JIMMY *enters from the room*]

JIMMY
[*Breathlessly*]
I'm here. I made it . . . What's happening? Where's every-
body?

CONNIE
Mike and Elizabeth just went off to the roller-coaster.

JIMMY
Together?

CONNIE
[*Nods*]
A minute ago.

JIMMY
That's strange. I thought they disliked each other intensely.
I thought they couldn't stand the sight of each other.

CONNIE
[*Indicating the rolled drawing that* JIMMY *is carry-
ing*]
What's that?

JIMMY
A drawing. I did it for Elizabeth. I'm giving it to her tonight.
Did they say they were coming back? What's taking them
so long?

CONNIE
They just went for a ride on the roller-coaster.
            [JIMMY *is looking around restlessly*]
I'll go tell them you're here.

JIMMY

Go on.
[CONNIE *still stands, waiting. She giggles*]
Go on, Connie. Get the lead out.

CONNIE

All right.
[*She runs upstairs, exits on the upper roof, right.*
JIMMY *follows, but stops on the upper roof as he*
hears MICHAEL *and* ELIZABETH *laughing. They enter*
under the bridge on the stage-level roof]

ELIZABETH

That was fun. That was really fun, Michael.

MICHAEL

It was, wasn't it? And you were afraid. I could see it in your
eyes.

ELIZABETH

Not of you.

MICHAEL

No?

ELIZABETH

No. I didn't realize how fast you go around those curves.
I was losing my breath.

MICHAEL

Somebody was holding on to me for dear life.

ELIZABETH
[*Smiling*]
You happened to be sitting next to me. I had no choice.

MICHAEL

You find me hard to take, don't you?

ELIZABETH

It's not that. We have different personalities. It's been that way from the first day we met.

MICHAEL

Do you think so?

ELIZABETH

Uhuh.

MICHAEL

I don't. I think our personalities are exactly the same. That's why we keep each other at arm's length.

ELIZABETH

Is that what you've been doing?

MICHAEL

Sometimes. Because I have the feeling, Elizabeth Evans, that if we ever got close to each other, very very close to each other, we'd both go up in a cloud of smoke.

ELIZABETH

You're conceited.

MICHAEL

The same as you.

ELIZABETH

And you're spoiled.

MICHAEL

The same as you.

ELIZABETH

And you think whatever you want in the world, all you have
to do . . .

> [MICHAEL *suddenly kisses* ELIZABETH. *A guitar starts*
> *playing a love ballad. Lights change.* MICHAEL *and*
> ELIZABETH *go off.* JIMMY *drops the drawing to stage*
> *level. Lights come up on* LEE HAINES *playing the*
> *guitar and singing*]

LEE

MY LADY HAS BLUE EYES,

SOFT HANDS, LONG HAIR, SWEET FACE.

SHE WEARS A SATIN DRESS,

AND A SLIP THAT'S MADE OF LACE.

> [JIMMY *walks over to the ventilator, left of the*
> *upper-roof door, where* LEE *is playing, and picks up*
> *a glass. The scene suggests a bar*]
> [*Speaking*]

San Francisco. That's the place, Jimmy Shine. Whatta you
got here? Nothin'. Nothin'. Cops and stiffs and cheesy joints.
But Frisco? Man, everything's swingin' out there . . . It
goes. It moves. It jumps. An' it's got the sweetest chicks.
Sympathetic chicks. I'm not puttin' you on, man. All the
creative cats make out in Frisco, even if you do jewelry or
ceramic work. Yeah. I do ceramic work myself. Ashtrays. An'
I'm livin' with four different broads an' I don't even smoke!
So whatta you say? You gonna come out?

> [JIMMY *puts down his glass, pulls out an empty*
> *pocket as he starts down the stairs, left, to his room*]

Money? Whatta you need money for? You get out on that
road and you put your thumb up, like this, and when those

cars go whizzin' by, you move it, you move it, like this, an'
you jus' keep goin' straight to the other end, straight to where
you start hearin' the seagulls cryin' an' flappin' around.

[*He starts to cross*]

An' when you get out there, you look me up. Lee Haines.

[*He starts to play the guitar*]

You look me up an' right away you got yourself a pad an'
plenty a' bread. You come on out, Jimmy Shine. And don't
forget. Lee Haines.

[*He sings*]

MY LADY LIKES TO SING,

TO LAUGH, TO PLAY, TO TEASE.

SHE ASKED ME FOR MY LOVE

AND THREW IT TO THE BREEZE.

    [JIMMY *is lying on the floor in his room, smoking
a cigar, his head resting on the stairs, left.* LEE *begins exiting on his last notes*]

CURTAIN

ACT II

[At rise JIMMY *is washing dishes, using the block of ice in the sink to wet the dishmop. He sweeps the floor, tucks his beret under the mattress, sweeps the bed, makes a line under the pillow with the end of the broom, and then takes off his apron, surveying the room as he does so*]

JIMMY

Sparkling.
[*He puts on his jacket*]
Never has the Shine apartment sparkled like it sparkles today.
[*He looks in the mirror*]
Hello, there, you handsome devil, you. Not looking too bad this morning.
[*He picks up an evening cane from behind the bed*]
Eyes a bit creased around the corners, but still young, still have a ways to go before it all falls apart, before it all . . .
[*His body slowly bends and he takes on the posture and voice of an old man. He moves to the door, playing an imaginary scene*]
Is that you there now, Elizabeth? Oh, one second, I'll be right there. Be patient . . . Legs a bit stiff this morning . . . Come in, Elizabeth, come in.
[*Opening an imaginary door*]
Oh, my Elizabeth. I am so glad you could come today. No, no, it's all right. I haven't been waiting too long. But let me look at you, my dear . . . You seem to have lost all your hair . . . no matter, no matter . . . Oh no, it is not the waiting that has upset me. It is my passion. My passion seems

to have slipped down to my knees, and our first attempts at
love-making may be a little awkward, but no matter, my dear,
we will work it out. Oh my dear, let us make love now, right
now . . . But first you must excuse me: I must go to the
bathroom . . .

> [*He checks the room once more, turns the flower
> right-side-up in the paint can*]

I'm ready for you now, Elizabeth. I'm waiting and ready,
Elizabeth Evans . . . Elizabeth Evans Leon . . .

> [MICHAEL *enters the door on the upper roof. A gui-
> tar is heard*]

MICHAEL

Jimmy, Jimmy, I have some wonderful, wacky news to tell
you . . . You're the first to know, word of honor. Elizabeth
Evans and yours truly . . . Are you listening, Jimmy? Are
are listening?

> [JIMMY *puts on a hat, picks up a paint box and
> canvases*]

Don't ask me how, buddy. Love strikes and resolution flies.
Period. That's it. We were married on Thursday. You should
have seen the hotel we stayed at . . . falling apart . . . it
was falling apart . . . Paint peeling, noisy bedsprings, no
service . . .

> [MICHAEL *exits. Lights come up on the San Fran-
> cisco area, on the lower roof, left, as* LEE *descends
> the stairs, singing. Others follow*]

LEE
[*Singing*]

MY LADY HAS BLUE EYES,
SOFT HANDS, LONG HAIR, SWEET FACE.
SHE WEARS A SATIN DRESS
AND A SLIP THAT'S MADE OF LACE.

[*Speaks*]

Hey! Jimmy!

JIMMY

Hi, Lee!

LEE

Welcome, welcome, welcome to San Francisco. Home of all that moves and grooves. There you go!

[*Presenting* JIMMY *to the group*]

Hey, all you cats and kittens. It is my sincere and happy pleasure to present, straight from the East Coast on his first and only visit to our fair city of Frisco, my old friend and one-time drinking pal, the original Jimmy Shine!

[*They shift to new positions; one boy claps unen- thusiastically*]

JIMMY

They're a real friendly bunch.

LEE

[*To the group*]

Tell him where it's at.

BOY I

We have walked the earth a thousand times.

BOY II

You said it, Daddy . . .

BOY III

Daddy . . .

BOY IV

Daddy . . .

GIRL I

Daddy . . .

ALL

Daddy . . .

GIRL I

And we have seen old men with big red noses . . .

BOY IV

Under the black moon we ask ourselves
What has happened to the red red roses?

BOY II

Stay with it, Daddy . . .

BOY III

Daddy . . .

BOY IV

Daddy . . .

GIRL I

Daddy . . .

GIRL II

Oh . . .

BOY I

Daddy . . .

GIRL III

Oh . . .

GIRL IV

Daddy . . .

ALL

Oh . . .
We have trudged many a weary mile
Searching among fossils for the thistle . . .
But all we find in the ashes and the rubble
Is a bare-assed nuclear missile.

BOY II

That's the way it is, Daddy . . .

BOY III

Daddy . . .

BOY IV

Daddy . . .

GIRL I

Daddy . . .

GIRL II

Oh . . .

BOY I

Daddy . . .

GIRL III

Oh . . .

GIRL IV

Daddy . . .

BOY II

Uh-uh . . .

ALL

Boom.

LEE

Beautiful! Beautiful!
> [*They settle themselves around the area.* LEE *puts
> his arm around* JIMMY]

Yeah, forget about all your troubles and get happy, man.
Good thing for you your chick ran off and married that
other cat.
> [*They sit on the rim of the lower roof, left*]

JIMMY

She wasn't my chick, Lee. She was just a close friend.

LEE

Yeah, yeah, yeah, yeah . . .

JIMMY

I mean it, Lee. I just had to get away for a while.

LEE

Well, you come to the right place, man; the one and only
place for true creative activity.

JIMMY

I really think I could do good work here, Lee. I'd like to do
a whole series on bridges. I'd like to paint every bridge in
San Francisco. Expressionistically. Using bright primary colors and . . .

LEE

Hey, slow down, man, slow down. You gotta learn to work systematically. You can't go rushin' into creative activity. Do you know how long it takes me to plan my ceramics? Those things don't just come to me. I gotta system.

JIMMY

What kind of system?

LEE

A system to keep your mind free and creatively clear. Now, I get up in the morning. And I have me two cups of black coffee, and I lay down in the bed and I look up at the ceiling, and I says to myself, "So what's bugging you today, baby?" And I think of all them things that's bugging me, and I go right back to sleep again.

JIMMY

That's not much of a system, Lee.

LEE

It's a great system, 'cause when I wake up, my head's filled with fantastic ideas. To date, using my system, I have sold exactly four thousand three hundred and seventy-five originally designed and conceived ashtrays . . .

JIMMY

Ashtrays . . . ?

LEE

Two thousand and six bowls, plates and platters, one hundred ninety-one string of beads, ninety-eight pair of earrings, and three sets of ceramic shoe buckles to a fag chiropodist.
[*Slight pause*]

JIMMY

Lee, do you ever think about dying?

LEE

Yeah, yeah, I think about it.

JIMMY

How do you handle it?

LEE

Well, I have me two cups of black coffee . . .
[*They laugh*]
Man, what you thinking about dying for? You got years to
worry about that.

JIMMY

I know, Lee, I know, but I can't get it out of my mind.
Sometimes I think if I don't make it as a painter, I'm going
to have to kill myself.

LEE

Man, what is all this talk about dying and suicide? A young,
good-looking cat like you . . . You just wait right there. I'm
gonna get you somebody who's gonna make you want to live
forever.

JIMMY

Who's that?

LEE

Millie.

JIMMY

Millie? Millie who?

LEE
Millie the Nymphomaniac.

JIMMY
[*Calling after* LEE *as he goes*]
You don't have to do that, Lee! I'm okay! I won't kill myself,
Lee, I promise! I . . . I . . .
> [*He is silenced by the appearance of* MILLIE *walking
> toward him, flat-footed, slouched. She is a tall, sex-
> less girl with long ink-black hair cut in bangs. A bell
> tinkles on a chain around her neck. She wears a long
> dark gown, no shoes*]

MILLIE
Lee's friend?
> [JIMMY *nods*]
I'm Millie the Nymphomaniac.
> [JIMMY *nods. Pause*]
I hate the name Millie.

JIMMY
[*Shrugs*]
It's not such a bad name.

MILLIE
I hate it. Vehemently.

JIMMY
It's nicer than the name Shirley or . . . Beverly.

MILLIE
I like the name Shirley. Shirley happens to be one of my
favorite names. If my parents had given me the name Shirley
instead of Millie, I would never have become nympho-
maniacal.

JIMMY
[*Shaking his head*]
Names don't influence us that much.

MILLIE
Oh, they do. Names do influence us, Johnny.

JIMMY
[*Slight pause*]
Jimmy. Jimmy Shine.

MILLIE
[*Shrugging*]
Johnny . . . Jimmy. I had a girl-friend once whose name was
Maxine. But everybody called her Max. It was Max this,
and Max that. Now she's running around with a girl named
Sammy.
[*Nods sadly*]
But what really disturbs me about having nymphomania is
that I get no thrill or excitement from doing it; sex is a
mechanical act for me. I just do it, mechanically.

JIMMY
Then why do you do it?

MILLIE
It's like eating peanuts. I can't stop.

JIMMY
You could if you made up your mind. I'm a painter, Millie.
A serious painter. And I know how to exercise self-control and
self-discipline and how to say to myself, "No. I will not do
this-and-this, I will do that-and-that." You have to say the
same thing to yourself, Millie. You have to say, "No. I will

not give in to temptation. I will not under any circumstances be degraded and used by dirty old men and degenerate creeps who have no feelings for me as a person."

MILLIE
[Firmly]
You're right, I know you're right. Oh, wow, you are so right!

JIMMY
You have to say that to yourself. And promise and swear that after today you will never, never go to bed with a man unless you're married to him.

MILLIE
After today?

JIMMY
I've become very fond of you, Millie.

MILLIE
But I want to start now, today.

JIMMY
[Excitedly]
But you don't have to start now, today! That's not self-discipline. Self-discipline is when you say to yourself, "To-morrow morning at eight o'clock sharp I'll stop doing this dirty thing, but up until eight o'clock sharp tomorrow morn-ing I'll do this dirty thing as much as I like." That's self-discipline!

MILLIE
[Rises, moves away]
No. I'm not waiting. I know myself too well, Jimmy. I have to start now, or I'll never make it.

JIMMY
[*Calling after* MILLIE *as she exits*]
Millie, wait a minute! Millie, don't make a decision you'll
be sorry for! Millie!!

LEE
What happened, man?

JIMMY
I just bombed out with a nympho!
[*Modern rock music starts.* LEE *sings, is joined by
the others.* JIMMY *tries to find a girl to dance with,
but they all have partners.* LEE *gets* JIMMY *to dance
with him.* JIMMY *sings a chorus. Military drum
beat, to which* JIMMY *and* LEE *march back from
the apron where they have been dancing. Music
ends*]

LEE
Hey, how's it going, man? Having a ball?

JIMMY
Yeah, I'm having a great time. You really swing, Lee. Wanna
go steady?

LEE
No, man, I'm already spoken for.
[MILLIE *crosses the room carrying a candle and wear-
ing an improvised nun's habit*]

JIMMY
[*As she disappears*]
Millie! My God, what have I done to you?
[*He picks up his paint box and canvases*]

LEE
What are you doing, man?

JIMMY
I'm sorry, Lee. I guess I don't fit in. I don't make this scene.

LEE
What's to make, baby? Just enjoy it.

JIMMY
No, I have to get back to New York. I have to go back home.

LEE
I told you, Jimmy, forget that chick.

JIMMY
I have to see what my friends are doing.

LEE
She's no good for you.

JIMMY
[Crossing the stage]
Thanks for everything, Lee.

LEE
[Exiting]
Forget her, man. Forget her, Jimmy. Jimmy!
        Lights come up on ELIZABETH. In this scene they're
        about twenty-five years of age]

ELIZABETH
Jimmy! Jimmy Shine!

[*Calls*]

Mike, Jimmy's here!

[*To* JIMMY]

Why didn't you phone and let us know you were coming?
You look good, Jim.

JIMMY

I feel good. I feel terrific. I finally saved up enough money
to get a new studio. It's down on Broome Street. A kind of
loft. In a factory building. I've been painting apples. A whole
series of big red Mackintosh apples. Symbolically. I've done
over forty apple paintings since I'm back.

ELIZABETH

You stay with it, don't you?

JIMMY

I brought you a present.

ELIZABETH

Are they all apple paintings?

JIMMY

All except the one for Mike: that's a tangerine painting.

ELIZABETH

Thank you, Jim, I'm sure we'll enjoy them.

JIMMY

How's married life, Elizabeth?

ELIZABETH

Hectic. But I do have a fur coat now. And a hat with flowers.
You remember?

[JIMMY *nods*. MICHAEL *enters*]

MICHAEL
Hey, you old son-of-a-gun. What's with you? Why didn't you let us know you were back?

[*Arm around* JIMMY]

How do you like the house, buddy?

JIMMY
Nice. It's really nice.

MICHAEL
Liz is looking great, isn't she?

ELIZABETH
Were you speaking about me, Mr. Leon?

MICHAEL
I most definitely was, Mrs. Leon.

ELIZABETH
Be my guest.

[*They kiss lightly.* JIMMY *moves underneath their kiss to the washtub chairs*]

ELIZABETH
Sit down, Jim. It's okay. They're chairs.

MICHAEL
Take mine, buddy.

[*Lifts* JIMMY *into a chair, 4½ feet from the floor; it swivels uncontrollably*]

They're from Liz's aunt. For middle-class suburbanites.

ELIZABETH
Mike's parents bought us the house.

JIMMY

Ohhhh.

MICHAEL

I told them not to. I didn't want it.

JIMMY

Boy, this certainly is a cozy chair.

MICHAEL

Hey, I've converted the attic into a studio. You have to see
it, Jimmy.

JIMMY

That's great! Then you're still painting.

MICHAEL

Well, buddy, at the moment I'm putting in over forty hours
a week at real estate.

JIMMY

Real estate?

MICHAEL

Well, I have to make a living. And I couldn't throw away
my father's business, could I? I'm not that mad.

ELIZABETH

Mike's father took ill . . .

MICHAEL

It's not that. I just don't believe that painters should have to
beg for handouts.

JIMMY

But you're not painting, Mike.

MICHAEL

Not now. Not this moment. I do have responsibilities.

ELIZABETH

Not meaning me, I hope.

MICHAEL

Meaning you and me. You working, Jimmy?

JIMMY

Uh-huh.

MICHAEL

Where? Doing what?

JIMMY

I thought you meant painting.

MICHAEL

I meant working, employment.

JIMMY

I work part-time. I'm a part-time expert.

MICHAEL

Well, whatever you do, stay off the unemployment line.
              [*Laughing it away*]
I'm paying enough taxes as it is.

ELIZABETH

I keep telling Mike he could go on painting if he'd let me go
back to work.

MICHAEL

As long as you're my wife, you're not working, period!

ELIZABETH

I think it's wonderful how Jim has managed to stay with it.

MICHAEL

Jim doesn't have a family to support.

JIMMY

That's true.

MICHAEL

Stay out of this, Jimmy.

JIMMY

Right.

ELIZABETH

Let him speak, Mike. What are you afraid of?

MICHAEL

Liz, I'm warning you.

ELIZABETH

Go ahead, Jim. I want you to speak, I insist you speak.
    [*Until they rise, they pull at* JIMMY's *chair so that
    he is forced to face the speaker*]

JIMMY

Fourscore and seven years ago our forefathers brought . . .

MICHAEL

You're staying for dinner, Jimmy. Connie's coming over.

ELIZABETH
Mike, there won't be enough. We can all go out.

JIMMY
Thanks anyway, Mike. But . . .

MICHAEL
I don't want to go out. Throw anything together . . .

ELIZABETH
I said, there isn't enough!

MICHAEL
Will you do as I—

ELIZABETH
Jimmy can come for dinner another time.

JIMMY
Forget it, Mike, I don't feel like eating.

MICHAEL
[*Glaring*]
Will you get us a couple of drinks, then? Or is that too
much . . .

ELIZABETH
[*Emphatically*]
In a minute. In one minute. I don't have to jump at the
precise instant you . . .

MICHAEL
[*Holds* ELIZABETH's *arm, not forcefully; to* JIMMY,
with embarrassment]

We have to have a drink together, Jimmy. We'll be right
with you . . .

JIMMY

Hey, Mike, I'm getting a little dizzy.
   [MICHAEL *and* ELIZABETH *have moved to the side,
   speak in loud vehement whispers*]

MICHAEL

For cryin-out-loud, will you let me know what you're trying
to prove?

ELIZABETH

You're the one who's trying to prove that you're the high and
holy master, that all you have to do is snap your fingers for
me to come running.

JIMMY
[*Shouting*]

Hey, I'm getting sick in here!

MICHAEL

Defensive about every goddam little thing.
   [*Slight pause*]
The fact that I'm not painting doesn't seem to mean any-
thing to you!

JIMMY

I'm gonna throw up all over the place.

ELIZABETH

Did I tell you to stop painting?
   [*Bell rings*]
Did I tell you to take over your father's business . . .

MICHAEL

You said. I said. I did it for the both of us, didn't I?
[They start to exit. CONNIE enters]

CONNIE

Elizabeth? Mike?

ELIZABETH

I'm not going to be taken for granted. I didn't marry you to
be less of a woman, but you want always . . .
[Sound of a door slamming]

JIMMY

Connie, will you get me out of here?
[CONNIE helps JIMMY out of the chair]

CONNIE

How are you, Jimmy?

JIMMY

I could be better.
[Shaking hands]
I've been meaning to call you . . .

CONNIE

I was hoping you would.

JIMMY

Let's get out of here.
[They move upstairs to the upper roof]

JIMMY

Connie, Connie, Constance Fry. What have you been doing?

CONNIE

Teaching. Fifth grade. In Flatbush.

JIMMY

Great.

CONNIE

You?

JIMMY

Painting.

CONNIE

I know that. Have you sold anything?

JIMMY

Not yet. I don't worry about it, though.
                [*Slight pause. He stares at her*]
I worry about other things lately.

CONNIE
                [*Blushing, turning away*]
Are you seeing anybody?

JIMMY

No. I . . . I've been too busy. You?

CONNIE

Nothing steady.

JIMMY

I was sure you'd be married by now.

CONNIE

I've been trying.

[*Laughing*]

Don't think I haven't been trying.

JIMMY

I'm glad.

CONNIE

Why?

JIMMY

I'd like to see you. I'd like to get to know you better. We've been friends for so long and we never even went out together.

CONNIE

You never asked me.

JIMMY

Mmm. So I'm asking you.

CONNIE

So I'm saying it'll be my pleasure, Mr. Shine.

JIMMY
[*Smiling*]

Great.

MR. LEPKE
[*Off, left*]

You're late, young fellow. You're late.

JIMMY

I have to go now, Connie. I have a new job.

[*He moves away. Lights fade from* CONNIE]

A high-class gallery on the East Side. Technical research and aesthetic evaluation of old master prints and paintings . . .

MR. LEPKE

[*Entering from the door on the lower roof, rear, cleaning the inside of a small barrel*]

You're late, young fellow, you're late.

[JIMMY *comes downstairs. During the following, he puts down his paint box, takes an apron from it and puts it on*]

It's about time. Fifteen minutes late and your first day in the fish business. That's no way to begin, no way to begin, I'll tell you that right now and I'll pick no bones about it. There's a right way and a wrong way and I can see right off that you're on the wrong way; took the wrong way the first day on the job, which is no small accomplishment considering the tough competition we got in this kind of work. And I'll tell you something else, young fellow . . .

JIMMY

Yes, Mr. Lepke, sir.

MR. LEPKE

I'll tell it to you gratis, man to man, straight to your face and no pussy-footing around the bush. There is money in fish, big money . . . if you know how to apply yourself; put your nose to the grindstone and learn the trade from the bottom up.

JIMMY

I would make every effort to do so, Mr. Lepke, sir.

MR. LEPKE

So listen to me, young fellow. Keep your eyes open, stay on your toes . . .

JIMMY

Yes, Mr. Lepke . . .

MR. LEPKE

. . . do what I tell you . . .

JIMMY

Yes, Mr. Lepke.

MR. LEPKE

. . . fill the orders . . .

JIMMY

Yes, Mr. Lepke.

MR. LEPKE

. . . show the ladies a little smile . . . Who knows? You
might turn out to be a natural.

JIMMY

Thank you, Mr. Lepke, sir.

MR. LEPKE

Turn around.

[JIMMY *does so*]

I got news for you, young fellow. You have the looks of a
fish man.

JIMMY

Thank you, Mr. Lepke, sir. But I only want this job part-
time. I'm a painter, a serious painter . . .

MR. LEPKE

Now, in this counter we have all the fish packed on ice to
keep them fresh and smelling nice. Smell any fish in here,
young fellow, huh?

JIMMY
[*Sniffing*]

A little bit, Mr. Lepke, sir.

MR. LEPKE

Well, it's late in the day, late in the day a little of that smell comes creeping up through the ice. But usually it smells in here like a flower shop. No fish smell at Lepke's. Now, here, young fellow, we have the carp . . .
[*He taps each "location"—flower pots, jars on shelf, cans, etc.—with a large machete*]
. . . pike, trout, flounder, squid, shrimp, eels and red snappers. [*After a slight pause* JIMMY *repeats his actions, borrowing the machete from him*]

JIMMY

Carp, pike, trout, flounder, squid, shrimp, eels and red snappers.

MR. LEPKE

Not bad. Not bad. Could you say, "How many seashells does little Mary Sweeney find on the seawashed southside seashore"?

JIMMY

"How many seashells does little Mary Sweeney find on the seawashed southside seashore?"

MR. LEPKE

"How many pecks does a woodpecker peck if a woodpecker pecks all day?"

JIMMY

"How many pecks does a woodpecker peck if a woodpecker pecks all day?"

MR. LEPKE
[*Sings, using the machete as a tuning fork*]

Do re mi.

JIMMY
[*Sings*]

Do re mi.

MR. LEPKE

Fa so la.

JIMMY

Fa so la.

MR. LEPKE

When you're in the fish business.

JIMMY

When you're in the fish business.

MR. LEPKE

Life is no easy matter.

JIMMY

Life is no easy matter.

MR. LEPKE

People don't realize.

JIMMY

People don't realize.

MR. LEPKE

How much you got to know.

JIMMY

How much you got to know.

MR. LEPKE

In fish.

JIMMY

In fish.
> [*They sing a vaudeville fish song, during which* MR. LEPKE *points out the benefits of being in the fish business. At the end of the song,* MR. LEPKE *sings out*]

MR. LEPKE

Let me hear it once more.

JIMMY
> [*Falsetto*]

Fish.

MR. LEPKE

Once more before I die.

JIMMY

Fiiiiiiiiish!
> [MR. LEPKE *kisses* JIMMY *on top of the head*]

MR. LEPKE

Now for the next step. Watch. Listen. Twenty years of experience in each move I make. First. We pick up an order. We read it.

JIMMY

We read it.

MR. LEPKE

And it says . . .

JIMMY

. . . it says . . .

MR. LEPKE

Mrs. Kay wants a five-pound trout. So . . . we take a trout
from the trout bin . . .

JIMMY

. . . trout from the trout bin . . .

MR. LEPKE

. . . we lay it on the scale . . .

JIMMY

. . . lay it on the scale . . .

MR. LEPKE

. . . and it says . . .

JIMMY

. . . it says . . .

MR. LEPKE

Five pounds.

JIMMY

Four pounds, six ounces.
    [MR. LEPKE *looks at him. He looks at* MR. LEPKE. *He
    looks at the scale*]
Five pounds.

MR. LEPKE

Right! Next step. Watch. Listen. We take the trout out of
the scale and lay it here on this wooden board gently, gently
. . . place this knife here, right here, directly beneath the
gills . . . we take this wooden mallet and gently, gently . . .
[MR. LEPKE *raises the mallet, about to hit the machete and decapitate the fish.* JIMMY *grabs his arm,
preventing him from swinging the mallet*]

JIMMY

Don't do it, Mr. Lepke!

MR. LEPKE

Don't do what?

JIMMY

Don't kill the fish.

MR. LEPKE

Who said I was killing the fish? I was just going to make him
a head shorter.
[*Shouts*]
Let go of my arm, young fellow.

JIMMY

I can't stand the sight of blood.

MR. LEPKE

Will you let go of my arm?

JIMMY

If you kill that fish, Mr. Lepke, I'm quitting!
[JIMMY *is still holding* MR. LEPKE's *raised arm which
holds the mallet.* MR. LEPKE *swings the machete
with his other*

hand, decapitating the fish. JIMMY *bends down to
make certain, jerks his head up at once*]

JIMMY

I quit!

MR. LEPKE

You're fired!

JIMMY

Good. I'm glad. I'm not spending my life chopping off fish
heads.

[*Takes off his apron*]

MR. LEPKE

You're a fool, young fellow, that's what you are. You could
have been a natural, a real natural . . .

[*He exits*]

JIMMY

[*Getting together his apron, jacket and paint box,
exits to the upper roof*]

I have to do one thing that makes sense. Before I lay down
and drop dead. Before I begin to stink like the fish . . . like
the . . .

[*To* CONNIE, *who enters, right*]

Connie, hi!

CONNIE

[*She is carrying a bag of groceries*]

Hi. How's your job?

JIMMY

Pretty good. I think I'm getting a promotion.

[*They enter* Jimmy's *room, down the right stairway.*
Connie *sets down the bag of groceries, not in the
room.* Jimmy *throws aside his jacket, apron and
paint box and lies down on the bed*]

CONNIE

Did you eat today?

JIMMY

I didn't have time . . .

CONNIE

If I didn't bring anything, you'd probably let yourself starve
to death.

JIMMY

Is there any soda?

CONNIE

Milk.
[*Takes a carton out of the bag*]

JIMMY
[*On the bed*]
Why don't you get comfortable?

CONNIE
[*Offers* Jimmy *a sandwich*]
Here. Take it.

JIMMY
[*Refuses the sandwich*]
I'll eat later. Come here, Con.

[CONNIE *hesitates, then crosses to a chair, stiffly, robot-like. She sits in the chair, folds her arms tightly*]

CONNIE

Do what you want with me.

JIMMY

Do what you want with me? The least you could do is either stand up or lay down!

CONNIE
[*Rises, moves out of room, right*]
I . . . I can't.

JIMMY

Why? Will you tell me why?

CONNIE

Because . . .

JIMMY

Because you don't care enough for me, right?

CONNIE

Do you believe that?

JIMMY
[*Getting dressed*]
What should I believe? That you want for us to see one another every day of the week and just remain platonic friends? That's impossible and you know it.

CONNIE

Why? We know each other long enough . . .

JIMMY

Be real, Connie, will you? I'm not spending my life playing
games. I don't have the time. I don't have the . . .

CONNIE

Do you want me to make you some soup?

JIMMY

Soup!

CONNIE

Some people do wait until they get married. Not everybody,
but there are some people . . .
[*Exits, carrying the groceries with her, rear right.
Lights change to present*]

JIMMY
[*Looking in the mirror*]
Under the circumstances, Constance Fry, it is better that
you go. We have absolutely no communication between us
whatsoever. And, after contemplating the matter at great
length, I conclude that you'd be a lot better off with someone
else. Someone who had a regular job and a regular salary and
all the fine accoutrements of a good, happy, joyful life.
[*He takes down a top hat which hangs from a peg
on the ceiling, does a W. C. Fields imitation*]
So go. Go, my darling honey-bun, go.
[*Picks up a cane*]
Heart-of-my-heart, dear old girl of mine.
[*Sings*]
Wedding bells are here again, wedding bells are here, are here
again, I'll be dead when you're gone, I'll be dead when you're
gone, you virgin-rascal you!
[*He coughs slightly, then turns it into an imaginary*

death scene. Lying on the floor, with the hat on his chest]

Is that you, Elizabeth? No, no, you didn't wait too long. Oh, Elizabeth, I'm so glad you're here. No more paintings of bones, no more fears, no more anxieties. Let me hold you, my Elizabeth. Oh, Elizabeth, let me make love to you just once, just once before I . . . But first, one request . . . Would you hand me the bedpan . . .

[JIMMY *puts the top hat on the can and twirls it around slowly, singing*]

"Gone are the days . . .

When my heart was young and gay . . ."

[*Present light dims*]

MICHAEL

[*Entering on the lower roof, rear*]

Jimmy, Jimmy, Jimmy, still fooling around, still playing games.

JIMMY

Come on, Mike, lie down next to me and we'll sing the old songs . . .

MICHAEL

Don't you ever get out of this place? It smells as if something's just died in here.

JIMMY

[*Sings*]

"Gone are the days . . ."

MICHAEL

[*Staring at a canvas*]

Still hung up on skeletons, huh?

JIMMY

That's a pigeon, Mike.

MICHAEL

I'll tell you this, and you can take it for what it's worth: I get
more of a kick seeing to it that people have adequate homes
to live in than I ever got playing around with paintbrushes.

JIMMY
[*Sings*]

"Gone are my friends . . .
From the cottonfields away . . ."

MICHAEL

Would you mind telling me how the hell you live?

JIMMY
[*Rises*]

I swear, Mike, you're becoming a bore. I get by. I had a job
last—

MICHAEL

A job, as what? An errand boy?
[*Takes out money*]

JIMMY

Put it away, Mike.

MICHAEL

Come on, Jimmy, don't be a fool.

JIMMY

You shouldn't do that; you shouldn't.

MICHAEL

It's nothing to me, for cryin-out-loud, take it!

JIMMY

Will you put it away! Why do you have to beat me over the head every time you come up to see me!

MICHAEL

Beat you over the head? I'm trying my damnedest to be of some use to you! I'm sorry, Jimmy, but from what I see of your work, you're going nowhere, fast.

JIMMY

I didn't ask for your opinion, Mike!

MICHAEL

Well, I'm giving you my opinion. Let's call it the prerogative of old friends. It's time you stopped deluding yourself. You didn't make it, so what? You're not the first, you're not going to be the last.

JIMMY

Thank you for your encouragement, Michael Leon.

MICHAEL

There's work for you in my office, Jimmy. A profession. You could wear a decent suit on your back, earn a decent salary. I can start you with . . .

JIMMY

Get off it, will you?

MICHAEL

All right, so you don't want to go into real estate. Agreed. I have friends in a number of professions who can give you a hand. How about commercial art? Advertising?

JIMMY

How about comic books?
[*He gets his paint box and a canvas*]

MICHAEL

Now, now, James Shine, don't get peevish. I'm only trying to help. You know, if I had decided to pursue painting as a career, I would have by now achieved some measure of success, some small measure of success, I daresay.
[*He puts on* JIMMY's *top hat, picks up the cane*]

JIMMY

[*Sitting on floor at the foot of the bed, staring at the canvas propped against paint box*]
Great. That's great.

MICHAEL

Because you know, Jimmy, you know I had talent. You know that, don't you?

JIMMY

Terrific! You had terrific talent.

MICHAEL

And I must say, after scrutinizing your works of art closely, very very closely . . .
[*He pokes at a painting with the cane*]

JIMMY

Mike, I'm really busy . . .

MICHAEL

I've come to the unavoidable conclusion, James Shine . . .

JIMMY

Don't touch it, Mike!

MICHAEL

That not only have you forgotten the elements of color and composition . . .
[*He pokes at the painting with the cane again*]

JIMMY

I said don't touch it!
[*He closes the paint box and starts to put it and the canvas under the bed*]

MICHAEL

But your paintings are incomprehensible. Ultimately and absolutely incomprehensible. And you have become, Jimmy-old-friend, a troglodyte, a recluse, a little old man, a morbid psychotic shadow . . .

JIMMY

Take off, Mike, take off!

MICHAEL

What, I ask you, what? What does it all mean?

JIMMY
[*Frantically, sketching on the floor with chalk*]
I have nothing to do with you any more. Nothing.

MICHAEL

What? What? What does it mean?

JIMMY
[*Fighting off the cane with which* MICHAEL *is prod-
ding him*]
Leave me alone! Leave me alone! Leave me alone! Leave me
alone! LEAVE ME ALONE!

ELDERLY GENTLEMAN
[*Opening the top half of the bathroom door*]
Between you and me, young man, what does it mean?

JIMMY
Mean? It's relationships, formal symbolic relationships. I'm
using shapes, lines . . .
[*A crowd appears on all parts of the stage*]

BOY
But what does it mean?

TWO GIRLS
What does it mean? What does it mean?

JIMMY
You see this object here . . . And this . . .
[MICHAEL *laughs. Others echo the laugh*]
But look, I'm working in other ways, too. By juxtaposing
opposites . . . by utilizing contrary elements . . . we arrive
at . . .

THREE MALE VOICES
An original Jimmy Shine!

SALLY WEBER
[*Opening the upper-roof door*]
He can do it every time!

*[Half the group laughs; the other half sings lines
from the auction song. JIMMY sings with them, then
plays both parts of a vaudeville act]*

JIMMY RIGHT

Tell me, Mr. Shine. Would you mind answering a simple
question?

JIMMY LEFT

No, not at all; go right ahead.

JIMMY RIGHT

Why don't you grab hold of yourself and look life straight
in the eye?

JIMMY LEFT

Look life straight in the eye? The last time I looked life
straight in the eye it was . . .
[MICHAEL laughs]
I . . . I couldn't . . .
[Others join in the laughter]

JIMMY

Right! That's right!
[Laughs desperately]
It's funny. It's not serious. It's a fantasy. Don't you see it?
Don't you get it?

ELDERLY GENTLEMAN

But what does it mean?

ALL

What? What? What does it mean?
[They whisper "What does it mean?"]

JIMMY

It's a vision, a private vision, a nightmare . . . and basically,
you see . . .

FEMALE VOICES
[Echo]

And basically, you see . . .

MICHAEL

Some people got it, some don't. That's how it is in this
cruel world.

[Laughter]

JIMMY
[Doing a desperate soft-shoe]

That's how it is in this cruel world.

MISS GREEN

James, will you please tell us what it means?

JIMMY

It means . . .

ELDERLY GENTLEMAN

What does it mean? What does it mean?

ALL

What? What? What does it mean?
[They laugh louder and louder]

JIMMY

It means . . . It means . . .
[He claps his hands over his ears. The stage goes
black. Silence. In the stillness]

It means we die. Do you understand that? It means we die.
[*Long pause. Lights change to present.* JIMMY *is seated on the floor, alone in the room*]

It means . . .
[*Singing quietly*]
"The toe bone connected to the ankle bone, and the ankle bone connected to . . . the Shine bone . . . and the Shine bone connected . . ."
[*There is a knock at the door which* JIMMY *doesn't hear. Another knock and* ELIZABETH'S *voice calls, "Jimmy, are you there?"*]

JIMMY
[*Gets up and goes to the door*]
Who's that?

ELIZABETH
[*Off*]
It's me. Open up.

JIMMY
Elizabeth? One second. I'll be right with you! One second!
[*He lights the fire under the kettle on the stove; tidies his clothes, smooths his hair in front of the mirror; finally he sniffs under his arm, then opens the door*]
Come in. Come in, Elizabeth. I didn't hear you . . .

ELIZABETH
[*Enters, carrying a suitcase*]
Were you sleeping?

JIMMY
No, no, I was . . . Let me take this . . .

[*He takes the suitcase, puts it in the alcove under the mirror*]

ELIZABETH

Thank you . . .
　　　[*He comes back to her. They look at one another*]
Hello, Jimmy Shine.

JIMMY

Hello, Elizabeth.

ELIZABETH

How have you been?

JIMMY

Hanging on.
　　　[*He crosses to the stove, zipping up his fly, embarrassed*]

ELIZABETH

I'm sorry for barging in, but everything's been happening so quickly . . .
　　　　　　　[*Looks around*]
So this is where you've been hiding out. I like it.

JIMMY
　　　　　[*Indicating a chair*]
Here. Sit down. Get comfortable. Wait a minute . . .
　　　[*He tears a bit of newspaper, puts it on the chair.
　　　ELIZABETH *laughs and sits*]
Can I get you anything? A cup of coffee?

ELIZABETH

I'd love it.

[JIMMY *spoons some instant coffee into a cup*]
Why didn't you ever phone? It must be over a year. Connie
married last August . . .

JIMMY

I heard.

ELIZABETH

How's the painting going?

JIMMY

I stopped. I took Mike's advice and tried to go straight. I was
fired from my fourth job last week. A warehouse. Loading
and unloading furniture. I'm in the best physical condition
I've been in years. So don't try anything funny, Elizabeth.

ELIZABETH

I'll let you make the first move.
[JIMMY *smiles*]
It's hard to believe you stopped painting, Jim. That's something I always admired you for: sticking to it. Why did you
stop?

JIMMY

I ran out of paint.

ELIZABETH
[*Laughing*]
I'm glad to see you, Jim.

JIMMY

I'm glad to see you, Elizabeth . . . You look great.

ELIZABETH

And you look . . . pale but promising.

JIMMY
[*Turning off the gas under the kettle*]
What's the suitcase for?

ELIZABETH
I'm leaving.

JIMMY
Where?

ELIZABETH
Denver. I have a reservation on the twelve-o'clock plane.

JIMMY
And Mike?

ELIZABETH
That's over. I wish I could say I'm sorry, but I'm not.

JIMMY
Isn't there any chance . . .

ELIZABETH
Not any more. I have a public-relations job waiting for me,
with one of the largest agencies out there. I was wondering
if you'd be interested in going with me.

JIMMY
[*About to pour water from the kettle into the cup*]
To Denver?

ELIZABETH
To Denver.
[ROSIE *opens the door.* JIMMY *pushes her out, shuts*

*the door—*ELIZABETH *does not see any of this.* JIMMY
quickly pours water into the cup, gives the cup to
ELIZABETH. *The coffee slops over; he uses the news-*
paper she was sitting on to dry off the cup]

JIMMY

Your offer took me by surprise . . . Are you really serious
about me going with you to Denver?

ELIZABETH

Why not? I'm tired of doing what's expected of me. I can
imagine Mike's reaction when he hears the two of us went
off together. Wouldn't that be something?

JIMMY

Is that why you want me to go?

ELIZABETH

Don't be silly. I couldn't care less what Michael Leon thinks.
If it doesn't work out, you can turn right around and come
back.

JIMMY

What if I said okay?

ELIZABETH

You mean that, Jim?

JIMMY

You really want me to go?

ELIZABETH

I really want you to go.

JIMMY

I guess I should get away for a while.

ELIZABETH

How long will it take you to pack?

JIMMY

Close your eyes and count to ten.

ELIZABETH
[*Closing her eyes*]
One, two, three, four, five, six, seven, eight, nine . . .
[JIMMY *pulls out a suitcase, opens it on the bed,
then looks around for something to pack.* ELIZABETH
*is counting and sipping coffee. Finally he goes to
the sink, gets some cans of beer and throws them
into the suitcase before she gets to "ten"*]

JIMMY
I'm packed.

ELIZABETH

You are as insane as ever, Jim.
[*She looks around the room, finds the chest of drawers, looks through the drawers until she finds one
with clothes in it, takes it out and puts it on the
bed. Through the following she packs the suitcase*]
Jim, I've rented a little house outside of town. You'll be able
to do all the painting you want out there. I'll be staying in
an apartment near the office, but we'll have weekends and
a couple of nights during the week together.

JIMMY

You really set it all up, didn't you, Elizabeth?

ELIZABETH

I thought you'd come.

JIMMY

Why did you wait until the last minute to ask me?

ELIZABETH

I didn't want to give you a chance to say no. I will have to
do some entertaining, but I'll do that in town. For a while
we'll have to keep this to ourselves. I don't want to antagonize anyone.

JIMMY

I would never antagonize anyone, Elizabeth. I make that
solemn promise to you.

ELIZABETH

As you can imagine, they're probably very provincial, so we'll
just have to be careful at the beginning.

JIMMY
[Putting on his "chest piece"]
I will be very, very careful. I will be extraordinarily careful.
I'll pretend I'm your gamekeeper.

ELIZABETH
[Laughing, takes the chest piece off his shirt and
packs it]
Will you stop teasing me! Everything'll work out fine, I'm
sure. I have a car we can use weekends . . .

JIMMY
[Breaks out in seemingly uncontrollable laughter]
It's really a funny bit, Elizabeth. After all these years . . .
the two of us . . . running off together . . .

ELIZABETH
[*Genuinely laughing*]
Isn't it? Isn't it, Jim?

JIMMY
And when Mike hears about it.

ELIZABETH
Can you imagine . . .

JIMMY
He'll . . . he'll scream his head off!

ELIZABETH
I wish I could be there to see it . . .

JIMMY
[*Suddenly grim*]
Is that why you want me to go?

ELIZABETH
[*Flustered*]
Jim, I . . .

JIMMY
To get even with Mike? Is that why, Elizabeth?

ELIZABETH
Jim, you're becoming impossible.

JIMMY
Why are you here?

ELIZABETH
Do I have to spell it out for you?

JIMMY

What's the sudden interest in me, Cookie?

ELIZABETH

I thought there was something between us. I thought you genuinely liked me. I didn't expect to come here and be cross-examined. That's the last thing I expected.
[*She sits, reaches for her handbag*]

JIMMY
[*Slight pause*]

Come to bed.

ELIZABETH

What will that prove?

JIMMY

I'll tell you later.

ELIZABETH

Ha! Ha!

JIMMY

You're very pretty, Elizabeth.

ELIZABETH

Thank you.

JIMMY

I used to say to myself—"Elizabeth is very pretty."

ELIZABETH

Then I wasn't wrong, was I?

JIMMY

But you've become tough, Elizabeth. You're a tough chicken now.

ELIZABETH

Is that bad?

JIMMY

Come to bed.

ELIZABETH

Come to Denver.

JIMMY

Come here.

ELIZABETH

We should go, Jim, or we'll be late.

JIMMY
[Putting his hand to her face]
Ever since I was seven years old, I always wanted to run away with Elizabeth Evans.
[He slowly lifts ELIZABETH out of the chair and starts dancing with her, humming the Handel piece, as she laughs and goes along with him. He dances her to the door and, in one motion, puts the suitcase in her hand and opens the door]

ELIZABETH

What's this?

JIMMY

Goodbye, Elizabeth Leon. I wish you all the happiness in the world.

ELIZABETH

You're not coming?

JIMMY

No.

ELIZABETH

I should have expected something like this. I'm not going to beg you, Jim.

JIMMY

Don't, sweetheart. It's not gonna help.
[*He kisses her on the cheek. She stares at him an instant, then exits.* JIMMY *closes the door, moves into the room. He gets a can of beer*]

JIMMY

You have to be very careful with women like that. They can turn on you in a minute and whoop! off go your badookas!
[*He drinks some beer, then goes to the bed and dumps the contents of the suitcase back into the drawer. He puts the suitcase away and turns on the pianola, which plays a variation on the fish song. He puts his painting apron on, takes the paintbrush can off the stove and puts it on the chair—the flower still in it—and checks the light on it. He gets a sketch pad, but drops it on the bed as the door opens and* ROSIE *enters*]

JIMMY
[*Throwing his arms out and shouting*]

Hey!

[*He turns off the pianola*]

ROSIE
[*Her hand out*]
Ten bucks, Jimmy. Let's have it.

JIMMY
Ten bucks.

ROSIE
Ten bucks.

JIMMY
You just walk in and say ten bucks.

ROSIE
Ten bucks.

JIMMY
You don't say hello.

ROSIE
No.

JIMMY
You don't say how are you.

ROSIE
No.

JIMMY
You just say ten bucks.

ROSIE
That's right. Ten bucks.

JIMMY

And you have the nerve to call yourself a businesswoman. You know, sometimes you make me so angry, Rosie, I don't want to have anything to do with you.

[*He puts the brush can back on the stove and checks* ROSIE *in the light*]

I want to give up and say, "Rosie Pitkin, forget it. You lead your life and I'll lead mine. Whatever love there was between us is now only a handful of ashes."

ROSIE

Look, Jimmy, I was nice enough to wait across the street until your sugar-baby left, now you be nice enough and give me my ten bucks.

JIMMY
[*Making her sit down in the chair*]
Sit down and shut up . . .

[ROSIE *is protesting*]
. . . and don't move and don't say another word!
[*He "threatens" her in mock Japanese*]

ROSIE

I'll sit here. I'll sit here all day. I'm not leaving until you give me my money.

JIMMY
[*Opens a beer and hands it to her*]
Drink.
[*Through the following he gets a piece of charcoal, picks up his sketchbook from the bed, and sits on the floor at the foot of the bed, facing* ROSIE]

JIMMY

How was your appointment?

ROSIE

How was yours?

JIMMY

Was he any good?

ROSIE

Terrific.

JIMMY

Better than me?
                    [No answer]
I'm talking to you, Rosie! Answer a person when you're being
spoken to!

ROSIE

Yeah, he was ten times better than you!

JIMMY

How could he be better than me?

ROSIE

He paid.
        [JIMMY gets up, gets the flower from the brush can,
        and gives it to ROSIE]
Would you mind tellin' me what we're doin'?

JIMMY

You don't deserve it, Rosie, but I'm gonna immortalize you.

ROSIE

How about just payin' me my money?

JIMMY

How about just shutting up and facing the light.
[*Takes his beret from under the bedclothes and puts it on*]

ROSIE

I thought you weren't a painter any more.

JIMMY

I don't want any more talking.
[*He starts to sketch, stops, looks at* ROSIE, *gets up and goes over to her, saying*]
Rosie, this is gonna hurt you more than it hurts me.
[*With a mock-Japanese command, he lifts the wig off her head*]

ROSIE
[*Screaming*]
You'll ruin my wig, Jimmy. If anything happens to it . . .

JIMMY
[*Placing the wig in front of a cup on the floor*]
Don't worry. I'm just going to feed it.
[*Fixing* ROSIE's *hair*]
You're not a bad-looking girl, Rosie Pitkin. Now you're beginning to look like something.
[*He sits with his sketchbook again*]

ROSIE
[*After a pause*]
Let me comb my hair . . .

JIMMY

Shh! Sit up . . .

[*She does*]

That's it.

ROSIE
[*After a pause, not turning her head*]

Jimmy?

JIMMY

What?

ROSIE

Don't make my nose too big.
[JIMMY *smiles, starts to sketch*]

JIMMY
[*Singing as he works*]

"Rosie . . . I'll paint your nose-y . . .
Rosie . . . Oh, Rosie mine . . ."

CURTAIN

MURRAY SCHISGAL

Murray Schisgal, Brooklyn-born, served in the Navy during World War II, performed as a musician with small jazz groups, practiced law for several years, then taught in public and private schools. His career as a playwright began with two one-act plays, *The Typist* and *The Tiger*, which were first produced in London and then, in a New York Off-Broadway production, won the Vernon Rice and Outer Circle awards. *The Tiger* subsequently was filmed from a scenario by Mr. Schisgal as *The Tiger Makes Out*. *Luv*, produced in 1964, was Mr. Schisgal's first Broadway success, and it too became a film. *Fragments* and *The Basement* have since been produced Off-Broadway, and for television he wrote *The Love Song of Barney Kempinski*. Other plays, *The Old Jew*, *Memorial Day* and *Windows*, have been produced throughout the U.S. and in Europe, and *The Chinese* has enjoyed a long run in Paris.